More Memories

of

Newcastle

upon Tyne

Edited by Bill Lancaster

*The publishers would like to thank the following companies for their
support in the production of this book*

Main Sponsor

Eimco (Great Britain) Limited

James Atkinson

British Engines Limited

Calder Industrial Materials

Colmil Plant and Equipment Company Limited

Walter Cox Limited

Stephen Easten Limited

Go North East

Hoults Estates Limited

Revol Limited

F Short & Sons Limited

Simpson Bros

White Bros. (N'cle-on-Tyne), Limited

Wingrove Motor Company Limited

First published in Great Britain by True North Books Limited
England
HX5 9AE
Telephone: 01422 377977
© **True North Books Limited 2000**

ISBN 1 903204 10 0

*Text, design and origination by True North Books Limited
Printed and bound by The Amadeus Press Limited*

Introduction

Nothing ever stays the same, and we cannot progress without change. Some changes, however, hurt more than others. Still remembered and mourned by many older residents of Newcastle, were the changes which had nothing to do with the Planning Department; it was the Luftwaffe who carried out the heartbreaking air raids on Newcastle in 1940 and 1941. Then there were the changes of the 1960s, when 'square box' skyscrapers and characterless office blocks began to replace the old arcades, banks, pubs and churches - many of which had been architectural gems. Swan House was built, and the Central

Motorway East was laid down to ease the city's growing traffic problem.

We are fortunate that the 20th century was so well chronicled, and this collection of fascinating images calls to mind the town as it was in our youth. We visit vanished places of entertainment such as the Cannon, which closed in 1990, and the Flora Robson Playhouse, which struggled for years against all odds, and sadly had to close down due to lack of financial support.

This new collection reproduces these and many more nostalgic images to remind us of the way we once lived. We hope that you will read and enjoy 'More Memories of Newcastle upon Tyne' - and remember that history is still in the making.

Contents

Action replay

James's Park on 9th March, had not been the greatest of times for the Magpies. Watched by a crowd of 54,000, the police had to move in to restore order during the match against Nottingham Forest while referee Gordon Kew called the players off the pitch for a full eight minutes. The violence - slated by the press as 'Football's day of shame' - resulted in 23 fans being hospitalised. The result was a 4-3 win for United (what linesman would have dared to suggest that Bobby Moncur's final goal was offside?), but after much debate the FA committee decided on a replay. The first replay at Goodison Park resulted in a 0-0 draw, but a goal from top shot Macdonald brought victory to the lads in the second replay at Elland Road. A 2-0 win at the semi-final at Hillsborough against Burnley put Newcastle on the road to Wembley. Who, looking at this set of memorable photographs, could believe that the Magpies had just suffered what had been labelled as 'the greatest humiliation in decades'? Defeat or not, the supporters were out in their thousands to greet the lads on their return.

This page: 'Howway the lads!' was the phrase on everyone's lips as Newcastle fans turned out in full force to welcome their team home from Wembley. It was 4th April 1974 - a day the club and fans alike will never forget. The season, marred by a pitch invasion by 300 fans at St

Both pages: Life's a game, but football is serious stuff. April 4th 1974 saw Newcastle and Liverpool in a nose to nose confrontation in the FA Cup Final, and thousands of Geordies converged on Wembley to cheer on their team. Kevin Keegan and Steve Heighway, however, kept the goals flowing during the second half and the humiliating 3-0 defeat sent Magpie fans spinning into shock. They had every right to show their disgust at Newcastle's poor performance, but they remained solidly behind their team. Tens of thousands descended on the station to give them the kind of welcome they could have expected had they brought home the coveted cup. As the team and officials took to their open-topped buses and toured the streets of Newcastle the cheers of thousands of supporters filled the air. Those who were there on that memorable day had seldom witnessed such a sight. As the parade progressed, some of the fans managed to walk alongside the buses, keeping pace with their heroes, while others grabbed the best positions they could, crowding into upper windows to get a better view. The city was carpeted with humanity, and echoing King Canute's fabled struggle against the incoming tide, lines of police officers held back the crowd to keep them from spilling into the path of the buses. What a day that must have been, not just for Newcastle United but for everyone who was part of the crowd - and that would surely have included many of our readers! Manager Joe Harvey, however, was one of the casualties, and he resigned in May 1975.

Memorable moments

The 1953 coronation was hugely popular in a Britain recently ravaged by war

The striking facade of Fenwick's store dominates this picture from 1953. It was taken to record some of the city centre decorations displayed that May and June which were put up to celebrate the coronation of Queen Elizabeth II. The centrepiece of the Fenwick's display was a 20ft image of the youthful Queen with the accompanying message 'Long may she reign' beneath it. The 1953 coronation was hugely popular in Britain as people had had precious little to celebrate since the end of the war. The enthusiasm and loyalty of the Queen's subjects in Tyneside was rewarded less than 18 months after the coronation when the newly-crowned Queen and the Duke of Edinburgh made an official visit to the region.

Above: Muffled up in warm coats, thick gloves, scarves and hoods, this party of school children waiting at Newcastle Airport to meet Harold Wilson were at last rewarded by being able to shake the famous man's hand. It was February 1967, and the reason for his visit was to open the new extensions to the airport. Newcastle Airport had been built in 1935, but by the 1960s the increase in air traffic meant that more facilities were badly needed. With a calculating eye to the future, a new runway, Instrument Landing System, Air Traffic Control Tower and Terminal Building were constructed, bringing the airport up to date. The new facility had everything that was state-of-the-art in 1967, and that year 360,000 passengers used the airport. Steady development of the facility meant that by the time Newcastle Airport celebrated its Golden Jubilee in 1985 it was showing record breaking returns. At the time of his visit, Harold Wilson was almost exactly half way through his first term as Prime Minister. Three years on he was to be ousted by Edward Heath when the Conservative Party was voted in once again.

*I*t is February 1965, and the clock mounted on the premises of the Northern Goldsmiths significantly reads 11am. Solemn crowds wait along Pilgrim Street, Northumberland Street and around into Blackett Street to pay their last respects to Winston Churchill, who had died on 24th January. Many who were in the crowd that day would have been thinking back to October 1951, when the great man visited Newcastle in person. That was an election year, and Winston Churchill was in the city as part of the Conservative Party's campaign. Then, they had lined the route along Grainger Street that Churchill's gleaming Rolls Royce would take, craning their necks to catch a glimpse of the great man whose familiar fat cigar and walking stick had, since World War II, become a patriotic symbol. As we know, the Conservatives won, albeit by a narrow margin, and at the age of 76 Churchill once more became Britain's Prime Minister.

Winston Churchill had seen war at first hand, and had been a war correspondent during the Boer War. After that he went into Parliament, holding various offices. In May 1940 he became Prime Minister following Neville Chamberlain's resignation. Churchill went on to lead the country and inspire the British people throughout the second world war.

Around the city centre

Above: Isn't it amazing how familiarity can breed, if not contempt, at least inattention? Few people passing the Royal Arcade stopped to admire the old building which, in January 1963, advises passers by to 'Travel by Blue Star Line'. Admittedly, the smoke blackened building looks more than a little past its sell-by date; the arcade, nevertheless, is widely recognised as one of Richard Grainger's masterpieces. In spite of its architectural magnificence, that part of Pilgrim Street was too far away from the main shopping centre. This, coupled with the fact that the building's rear entrance was situated in less than salubrious Manor Chare, meant that few of those shoppers who had any real money to spend actually spent it in the Royal Arcade! By the date of our photograph the building's days were numbered. Not too far on it would make way for 20th century progress as Swan House and the huge roundabout were constructed. It was a bleak, wintry day when our photograph was taken; snow slides and drips miserably from the rooftops, while on the ground it has been reduced to a layer of dirty slush. The few pedestrians unlucky enough to be passing along Pilgrim Street at the time are undoubtedly looking forward to a hot meal and a warm fire.

Courtesy of the Ward Philipson Collection

Right: A scene dominated by the imposing, smoke-stained stonework of St.Nicholas Buildings reminds us of how this busy thoroughfare leading from the city centre to the High Level Bridge once looked. We are reminded too of a time when parking restrictions were not as overbearing as they are today. Some of the motors in this picture almost look as if they had been abandoned with not a yellow line, parking meter or Traffic Warden in sight! The picture dates from 1952, just about 100 years after the fine Italianate building was constructed. During the painful process of city centre redevelopment in the 1960s and 1970s many fine old properties like St.Nicholas Buildings were swept away in favour of modern, purpose-built retail units and office blocks. St.Nicholas Buildings escaped this fate but was the subject of extensive redevelopment in the mid 1990s which saw all but its impressive facade rebuilt. Other buildings were not so lucky, standing empty and unwanted for decades, often in a state of shameful disrepair, with broken windows and grass-filled gutters causing embarrassment to their modern well maintained neighbours.

Below: The annual Lindisfarne concert has been an institution in Newcastle ever since the long ago days when the group made 'Fog on the Tyne' a national hit, and people of all ages across the country went around whistling and humming the song. This fascinating view was captured in December 1981 as the concert-goers gathered outside the City Hall and formed an orderly queue that stretched around the building. Were they all ticket holders, we wonder - or were the people in the queue merely trusting to luck? If so, those near the end of the queue would doubtless have been on tenterhooks, hoping against hope that they would be able to find a seat when at last it came to their turn! Closer inspection of the photograph reveals that the majority of people in the shot are young people intent on enjoying their Christmas treat. The Lindisfarne Christmas Concert is an established tradition which was carried on even after the tragic death of Alan Hull, and remains a festive treat eagerly anticipated by Newcastle's music lovers.

otorists who are used to driving in today's hectic traffic conditions often look back with nostalgia to the 'good old days' of the 1950s and 60s when there was comparatively little traffic on the roads. It takes photographs such as this one to demonstrate just how short our memories are! It was the build up of vehicles in the city centre and the resulting congestion that called for the urgent action which led to the sweeping changes of the mid 1960s. John Dobson Street was laid out, alleviating the demands on Northumberland Street; the new Central Motorway cut a swathe through the city, and the Pilgrim Street Roundabout swept away many old and familiar buildings. Our photograph is dated 19th September 1961, and the view captured looking north along Pilgrim Street would within a few short years change out of all recognition. The Royal Arcade on the right was one of the many casualties of progress. The scene brings back memories of the lorries that were typical of the day and the vehicles we once drove. Is the car in the foreground a Vauxhall Victor? Its identity might not be too clear, but certainly the rather nice vehicle to its left is a Mk 2 Jaguar.

with the endless gifts we are expected to spend hundreds of pounds on. We would not wish for a return to the poverty that marked the early years of the 20th century, when Santa left few if any gifts in children's stockings - but oh, for a return to those simple, non materialistic Christmases!

Top: The sight of numbers of taxis outside Central Station has never been an unusual one. But taxis deliberately causing an obstruction and blocking the main station portico, and police officers engaged in arguments with the taxi drivers, certainly is. The date was September 1968, and the taxi drivers were involved in a bitter dispute with the local authority about their monopoly of the trade. Taxis have been as common as sparrows since Queen Victoria opened the station back in 1850 - the only difference being upon the horsepower of the vehicles, which was of the four legged variety in Queen Victoria's day. The taxi drivers' protest about the monopoly in 1968, in the event, failed.

Above: Christmas shopping; you either love it or hate it - but you still have to do it! Every shop you enter glitters with tinsel, Christmas trees and gifts, but it's after dark that Newcastle comes to brilliant life with hundreds of coloured lights that sparkle like gemstones in the darkness. This spectacular view of the city centre, snapped in December 1969, captures the flavour of the festive season.
In today's commercially-minded society, Christmas trees, coloured lights and elaborate decorations find their way into the shops around the end of September, along

Above: The Victorian politician W E Gladstone, who was four times British Prime Minister, once described Grey Street as 'England's finest street'. His opinion has been echoed many times down the years by those who have stood and marvelled at the magnificent Theatre Royal, whose Corinthian portico can be seen on the far right of our photograph, the Central Exchange, the Northumberland and District Bank (which became Lloyds Bank), and the frontage of the Royal Turks Head Hotel. Thankfully, Grey Street's elegant architecture survived the red pen of the 1960s planners - though back in 1899 the Theatre Royal had a narrow escape when a devastating fire destroyed its magnificent interior, leaving the theatre a burnt out shell. It was rebuilt by the well known theatre designer Frank Matcham and reopened in 1901. Further renovations were carried out in the late 1980s. The Royal Turks Head Hotel on the left was redeveloped in the early 1990s and is today a bank. Lines of rather nice cars are parked at the kerbside in this view which dates from

April 1974 - as they still do today. We note that there is some slight congestion in the street caused by a number of motorists who are no doubt wondering why, in an expanding universe, they can never find a parking space!

Below: Amazing, isn't it, that if your car is going to break down it always seems to do it in the worst possible place? Give a car a length of road and the engine will cough its last on the roundabout at the end of it. This kind of embarrassing situation has developed at the traffic lights in Pilgrim Street, though an alternative explanation could be that the car has been involved in a minor collision. Surely the young lady driver has not merely halted the progress of S Russell & Co's lorry in order to ask this long suffering police officer how to get to the A1? A quick thinking photographer took out his camera and recorded the scene for us back in April 1965. Readers will recognise and have fond memories of the old Ford Anglia on the left of the photograph; the inward sloping rear window made the design memorable. Was the Anglia perhaps your own first car?

This page: By the late 1960s parts of Newcastle resembled a huge building site. Readers who were motorists at the time will never forget the building of the Swan House Roundabout and the city's new motorway system! Swan House, seen here in the process of construction, was originally built as the GPO telecommunications headquarters *(bottom)*. The sheer size of the site, and the mammoth building with its massive supporting piers, is breathtaking. But constant change, so they say, is here to stay, and by the dawn of the 21st century the building stood empty, and rumours were being tossed around about its being turned into a hotel. Only time will tell....
Richard Grainger's Royal Arcade, built in 1831-32,

had to be demolished to make way for the building of the new office block. As a shopping arcade, the scheme was a commercial flop as it was built in an unfashionable area of the town, and it never became very popular among more affluent shoppers. By the 1880s, demolition of this architectural gem was already being talked about, and the deed was finally done in the early 1960s. A replica of the arcade - vilified as a ghastly imitation by most who had seen the original - was built underneath Swan House.

Our second view was recorded as the new round-about emerged from the rubble of the construction sites *(below left)*. Mosley Street, on the left of the

photograph, leads off towards the A1 south; Charlton's Brass Works in the background, along with most of the other older buildings seen here, were later demolished. There was little traffic on the roundabout when the photographer recorded the scene on 28th May 1968; the little VW Beetle on the right was one of the most popular cars of the time. As the 1960s swung into flower power the Beetle became the perfect statement of the young. Small and inexpensive to run, the Beetle was a car that dared to be different - even VW's own ads poked fun at it! Owners saluted each other as they passed - ownership almost became a club. This, the most popular car in the world, was the car that refused to die.

Above: Spot the missing element in this photograph.... It was April 1968, and the lack of buses gives us a hint that a total of 1,400 corporation bus drivers were on strike at the time. Blackett Street was empty of all but private cars, and there are remarkably few of them about in this interesting shot. The lack of traffic has brought a few jay walkers out, though they still need to be wary if they want to avoid looking at flowers from the wrong end.... The umbrellas, puddles and flogging windscreen wipers tell us that this was hardly the best date that could have been chosen for a bus strike; the end of the day would see a host of tired and dejected workers making their way damply home with sore feet and shortened tempers. This scene has changed almost beyond recognition today. The rather nice YMCA building was built in 1896, and is typical of the ornate and solidly respectable Victorian architecture that was common at the time. What would its designer make of the Eldon Square Shopping Centre which would one day replace it, we wonder?

Right: Before construction of the new Pilgrim Street Roundabout could begin, the existing buildings - Richard Grainger's Royal Arcade - had to be demolished. Back in 1830, Grainger's first plan had been to build a corn exchange in Pilgrim Street; his plans were thwarted by the Town Council, who rejected his plan, so he decided on a shopping arcade instead. The beautiful new building, with its handsome vaulted ceiling and eight glass domes, proved to be one of his masterpieces. It housed both offices and shops as well as important services such as the Post Office and a number of banks - not to mention the steam and vapour baths. The shopping arcade, however, was never very successful, and by the turn of the 20th century it was in decline. The Royal Arcade was demolished and by 1965, the date of our photograph, work on the new Swan House Roundabout was gathering pace. The Holy Jesus Hospital can be seen in the background; future years would see it become the Joicey Museum, which itself would eventually close, and the new millennium saw the ancient building, constructed in 1681, standing empty.

Below, both pictures: Fire hoses snake along Northumberland Street, a pall of smoke rises into the sky, and Christmas illuminations droop forlornly across the street, their festive spirit extinguished for ever. The greater - and far more tragic - illumination comes from the brightly lit shop windows. Their splendid displays are doomed as fire takes hold and spreads fast from floor to floor of the building. In the well-lit windows of Van Allan, dummies model the latest styles - the knee length skirts that were still the height of fashion at the time - but the firefighters' gaze is towards the upper floor, where one of the crew works from the top of the tender's extending ladder, training his jet of water on the seat of the fire *(bottom)*. The number of hoses, coiled like a mass of writhing serpents, reveal the extent of the devastating blaze. Hours of desperate work from the fire crews working with their long lines of hose, ladders, extensions and high pressure jets of water could not

save Callers from destruction.

The date was December 1969, and Callers, one of Newcastle's favourite stores, was left a burnt out shell. And after the fire was out and the damage estimated, there were big decisions that had to be made. For those left counting the cost after the mopping up operation, that Christmas could not have been a happy one; the eventual outcome we know already - the building was later demolished and today a well-known record shop occupies the site.

*A*steady trickle of traffic makes its way along Percy Street, while a row of sun blinds protect goods on display in the shop windows along Blackett Street, leading off towards the top right of the photograph. The eye follows the natural line of Blackett Street and up towards the Grey Monument, which eagle-eyed readers should be able to pick out in the distance. Eldon Square, a quiet retreat amid the bustle of the city, is a pleasant, tree-shaded garden where back in 1962, the date of the photograph, you could sit for a while, read your newspaper, eat your lunchtime sandwiches or just relax in the sun and let the world go by. By the 1990s the often vandalised wooden seats had gone, as had so much of the surrounding area. The war memorial, a statue in bronze of St George in the act of killing the fabled dragon, is thankfully still there. Designed by Charles Hardman, the Memorial was unveiled in 1932.

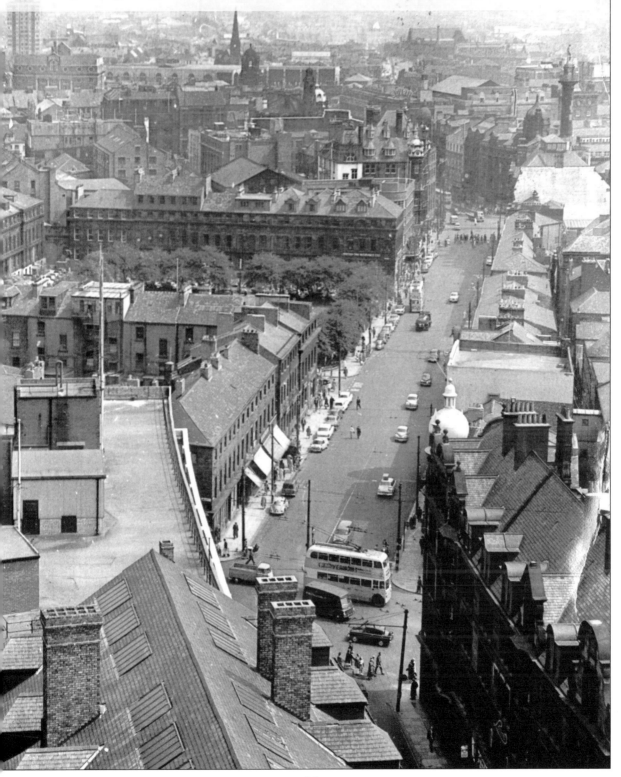

This page: A couple of long and not too robust looking ladders inform us that repairs of some kind were in progress at the Guildhall when a photographer stopped to record the occasion back in September 1938 *(below centre)*. Readers will perhaps note the missing element - there is a distinct lack of workers in this scene of suggested industry! The time, however, might give us a clue: at ten minutes to three in the afternoon we might expect that the workers have downed tools and were, at the moment this photograph was taken, sitting down with a mug of hot tea. The date is significant; in 1938 the clouds of war already hung low over the country and preparations were being made. Local air raid precautions organisations were established in every district and air raid wardens appointed and trained - and the Home Office prepared a booklet entitled 'The Protection of your Home against Air Raids', which was sent to every home in Britain. Almost 30 years on, more radical restoration work is being done on the Guildhall *(above)*. Clad in an exoskeleton of scaffolding, the historic building is undergoing a much needed facelift, and this time we can detect a few workmen dotted around the site. Readers with a sharp eye will spot the fact that they are not wearing the safety helmets which are obligatory on any site today, when 'No hat, no boots, no job' is the order of the day. The massive piers of the High Level Bridge can be seen in the background of this second photograph, dated 16th June 1966.

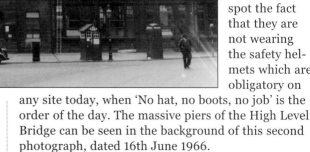

This page: The job is done and applause is in order as the flag is raised above the brand new regional government office complex, Wellbar House. It was the summer of 1962, and as the sun shone down on the workers it was time for them to relax with a frothing pint of Newcastle, give themselves a well-earned pat on the back, and smile cheerfully for the camera as these scenes were recorded for posterity.

The Sixties were swinging, and the only way was up as architects raised their eyes to the sky, sharpened their pencils and took out their slide rules. The new trend was towards soaring office blocks such as Wellbar House. Housing, too, was heading skyward as whole areas of old housing were cleared to make way for motorways and new development schemes, and tower blocks like those built in Shieldfield - prominent in the background of the photograph - were seen by many as the way forward. For many of the new residents, however, the new blocks seemed like filing cabinets for people, and looking back with the perfect vision of 20/20 hindsight we can appreciate that the old community spirit was often missing in this new environment. The friendliness of neighbours who were always ready to step in with the loan of a cup of sugar in an emergency, or a little sympathetic help and advice in a family crisis, had gone - perhaps for ever.

Below: The new emerges alongside the old as the face of modern Newcastle develops. This was August 1962, and we can see that the Civic Centre, in the background of the photograph, was still under construction at the time. Though the design for the building was chosen by competition back in 1939, the actual construction did not begin until 1950. The Centre dwarfs St Thomas' church, situated not far away in the Haymarket. Another landmark well worth a mention is the old synagogue in Leazes Lane which younger readers will today know as the Leazes Arcade. John Johnstone designed the building back in 1880, and in 1990 a disastrous fire almost put paid to the historic building. Workmen eventually moved in and by 1996 the old building had been restored and given a new lease of life.

Right: Apart from the lady bearing a bag in each hand, there were little signs of life outside the County Hall when this scene was shot back in 1965. Though on close inspection the many storeyed building has a number of attractive features (and could be labelled 'imposing' by those more qualified to judge), the massive structure, opened in 1934, nevertheless carries a forbidding air of solidity, and seems almost to frown down on its immediate environs. The County Hall, designed by local architects Cackett, Burns Dick & Mackellar, was built on the foundations of an earlier building which dated from 1910. A change of use later gave the building a different character and we know it today as the Vermont Hotel.

Below centre: The area around the foot of Grey's monument resembles a rubbish tip, and the great man himself gazes impassively down on the scene from his 135ft perch high above the scene. The photograph is dated 23rd January 1973, and the new Metro underground station was in fact in the process of being built at the time. The imposing column was erected in 1838 to commemorate the passing of the Great Reform Bill in 1832. Charles, Earl Grey, was responsible for the passing of the parliamentary reform act which gave the vote to merchants, businessmen and well to do farmers (though not to the ordinary man in the street - and votes for women still lay many years in the future). The 13ft statue of Earl Grey - the creation of Edward Hodges Baily - was brought to Newcastle by ship from London and winched to its position atop the column. Few have seen the statue at close quarters, and fewer still would detect that the head is by a different sculptor; Ralph Hedley gave Earl Grey a new head in 1941, though it was a thunderstorm rather than an enemy bomb which dislodged the original.

Bottom: Virtually every respectable town and city had a Burton's gents outfitters - and Newcastle was no exception. The distinctive white-stone facade was recognisable everywhere and became as much a part of the Burton's image as the distinctive gold-on-black lettering which adorned each of their stores. The popularity of suits, jackets and overcoats during many decades, along with Burton's ability to produce them at affordable prices, led to rapid growth and burgeoning wealth for the company. The firm's shrewd owners invested heavily in bricks and mortar in the form of purpose-built stores in prime commercial locations such as this one. In later years the attractiveness of this particular site was to prove its undoing as this Burton branch was pulled down to make way for the Monument Mall Shopping Centre. On the left of the picture it is just possible to make out the impressive clock which marks the location of Northumberland Street's well-known jewellers, Northern Goldsmiths. The beautiful golden lady has stood with optimistically-outstretched arms on top of the clock since 1932.

Courtesy of the Ward Philipson Collection

sick and elderly residents, the Maison Dieu. Trollope's building included markets - the fish market was situated beneath the colonnades of the elegantly curved building, which were open at that time. John Dobson reconstructed the Guildhall in the 1820s and blocked in the open fish market, resulting in the building we know today.

Top: Long before anyone even thought of pedestrianising Northumberland Street a convoy of flat-backed lorries can be seen snaking its way down what was to become one of the busiest shopping areas in the whole of Britain. The scene dates from around half a century ago, July 1952, recording a proud moment in the history of one of Tyneside's better known firms, Scott and Turners.

The company, based at the well-known Tin Box Factory, had won a massive export order for one of their famous brands - Andrews Liver Salts, and 140,000 tins of the highly

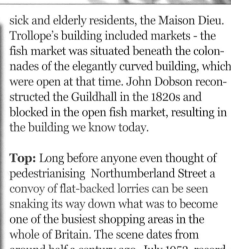

Above: The Guildhall is looking a little forlorn and rather the worse for wear in this photograph, which dates from December 1962. It was taken just a few days before Christmas, in fact, but the rather bleak scene contains no sign of festive cheer, and without so much as a Christmas tree in sight it could have been recorded on any day of the year. Four years on, the building would be receiving a needed facelift. The Guildhall - one of Newcastle's most historic buildings - has been through many changes in its long life. Designed by Robert Trollope, it was built in 1655, and incorporated an even older building, a hospital for

effective remedy were paraded through the city before being shipped to Canada. The export order was welcome news for the British economy which was practically on its knees under the burden of the massive national debt carried over from the second world war. During the 1950s industry was encouraged to export its products where possible in preference to satisfying tyne considerable demand in domestic markets. Consequently many products were in short supply in Britain. Younger people are often surprised to learn that wartime rationing did not completely end until July 1954.

Left: So much has changed since this view of the quay was captured back in November 1975 that it's difficult to know where to start! Not least is the number of vessels moored here. These were Scandinavian vessels assumed to have been sheltering in Newcastle from the North Sea storms. The truth - so the story goes - is that the Scandinavian seamen were taking advantage of the devaluation of the pound and were here to do their Christmas shopping! Scandinavian ships were regularly seen in Newcastle; our photograph shows the long row of butter sheds on the quayside, used for the imports of Danish and Swedish butter. The large, square building in the background behind the butter sheds was at the time of the photograph the CWS warehouse, built around the turn of the 20th century. The warehouse was converted to a hotel during the redevelopment of the Quayside and is today the Hotel Malmaison. The tall warehouses to its left in the photograph were converted into luxury flats, while the building to its left was eventually demolished for the building of the Crown Court in the late 1980s.

By the riverside

Below: This lone workman would appear to be courting disaster as he sits in the middle of the road, vulnerable to every passing truck. On any normal day he would indeed stand a good chance of ending up looking at the flowers from the wrong end, but when this fascinating image was recorded the traffic had been diverted so that repairs to the Tyne Bridge could be carried out. It was January 1965, so the day would no doubt have been a chilly one for hanging around. The workman, however, doesn't appear to be too worried by the recent rain, and when it's time for lunch he is quite content to down tools, knock off for an hour and take the weight off his feet. As long as he has his flask of hot coffee, a packet of sandwiches, and the morning paper to browse through, the miserable weather is not going to upset him too much. We might stop to wonder, though, where the rest of the gang had got to. The nearest warm pub, perhaps?

Above: The aptly named Ship Inn, dwarfed by the towering cranes and the bulk of a new vessel under construction, was doubtless the first port of call at the end of a long, hard day, and we can imagine numbers of thirsty workers calling in as they passed on the way home for a much needed glass of Drybrough's. We have no date for this view of the Ship, on Oil Mill Road, Low Walker, but a little detective work reveals that the photograph must have been taken early in the 20th century. The pub adjoining Swan Hunter's Yard was acquired by W B Reid, who rebuilt the establishment and changed its name to the Neptune Hotel in 1908. The Neptune Hotel was not merely a hotel in name; the smart new concern offered good class accommodation and was quickly adopted by the more affluent ships' captains who would stay there while their vessels were undergoing a refit. The Neptune Hotel closed in 1976.

Above right: Construction of the Tyne Bridge was still in progress when this magnificent view was captured for posterity. The arch of the bridge curves elegantly away from us - at the time a great design coup for the city, as the Tyne Bridge had the largest arch anywhere in Britain. It is often compared with Sydney Harbour Bridge in Australia; tenders were accepted and contracts were signed for both bridges during 1924, though the Tyne Bridge was opened in October 1928 and Sydney Harbour Bridge in March 1932. In their admiration of the bridge itself, many fail to appreciate the pairs of Cornish granite towers which support the bridge at each end. Designed by the well known Newcastle architect Robert Burns Dick, the impressive twin towers remind one of the medieval castles of long ago. The opening of the bridge in 1928 was a red letter day in Newcastle, and there was a holiday atmosphere among the motorists who came from far and wide to cross the bridge, delight in its impressive soaring archway, and admire the scenery from the new viewpoint far above the river.

Below: Tall cranes dominate this impressive scene as they rise above the Naval Yard at Low Walker, bringing to mind the terrifying alien invaders in 'The War of the Worlds'. From Newcastle's earliest years its position on the River Tyne has gone hand in hand with its local industries, especially coal, which has been mined in the area since Roman times. By the Middle Ages the town already had a thriving export trade with London and the Continent, and ships were being repaired and refitted in Newcastle. Walker has been a traditional shipbuilding area for many years; Hawthorn Leslies, one of the world's leading shipbuilders, moved into Walker in 1872. By the turn of the 20th century the industry was buzzing, and the famed 17,000 ton Mauretania - the largest vessel to be built on the Tyne - left Swan, Hunter and Wigham Richardson's yard in September 1906. Foreign competition was largely responsible for the decline in shipbuilding on the Tyne during the 1950s, and sadly, Swan, Hunter were one of the casualties.

Bottom: The story of Newcastle's Swing Bridge takes us back to the mid 19th century, and the days when a Georgian stone bridge crossed the Tyne at this point. Seagoing vessels, of course, could go no further than the bridge, which did not matter too much until W G Armstrong's Elswick Works began to expand and develop. The engineering firm originally built hydraulic machines, but as the company extended their operations into ship building and armaments the stone bridge presented a real

problem. Designing and building a new swing bridge was grist to Lord Armstrong's mill, and as the Tyne Improvement Commissioners set about demolishing the old one and erecting a temporary bridge, Armstrongs constructed the new double cantilevered 1,200 ton bridge. Originally driven by steam (though replaced by electric pumps in 1959), the hydraulic machinery pivoted the bridge through 180 degrees to allow for the passage of ships - and appropriately the first ship to use the bridge was bound for the Armstrong Works. The construction of the new Swing Bridge took eight years, and it was opened on 15th June 1876, though no special ceremony marked the occasion.

Aerial views

uilt during an era when harsh angles, geometric designs and hard lines dominated architectural design, Wellbar House rose to tower above the old streets and shops below, much out of place as Santa Claus in July. Many ﹍ders will perhaps agree that one of the best things ﹍ut the new tower blocks which began to spring up ﹍nd Newcastle during the 1960s was the view ﹍ss the rooftops of the city that could be had from the top of them! In this view which today is dominated by the Eldon Square Shopping Centre, Blackett Street leads away from the centre foreground of the view. Eldon Square, whose classical buildings graced Newcastle from the second quarter of the 19th century, was still intact at the time of the photograph, though by 1970 the north and west sides of the original square had disappeared to make room for the new shopping complex.

Courtesy of the Ward Philipson Collection

Left: This dramatic gull's eye view of the city and the river was captured on 19th October 1965, and shows three of Newcastle's most important bridges. On the left, the curve of the railway line leads us into the photograph and crosses the Tyne by way of the High Level Bridge, opened in 1849 by Queen Victoria. Built to carry rail traffic on the upper deck and road on the lower, the High Level Bridge, designed by Robert Stephenson and T E Harrison, was not only the first of its kind in the world but also had the longest spans. Less than 30 years later, the Swing Bridge in the centre photograph replaced a Georgian stone bridge which had been a severe handicap to seagoing vessels. The third of the bridges, the Tyne Road Bridge, was the last of the three to be built; it was opened by King George V in 1928.

Above: The Haymarket War Memorial, built to commemorate losses endured in the South African war, acts as a focal point for this interesting aerial view which dates from 1957. To the left of the traffic island upon which the memorial stands is the green and leafy oasis surrounding St Thomas's Church. By the time this photograph had been taken St Thomas's had been standing in the Haymarket area for 127 years, being completed in 1830. Decades of exposure to the smoke from industrial and domestic chimneys, not to mention fumes from the daily stream of motor traffic on adjacent roads, had stained the walls of this fine old building jet black. Across the way a handful of buses await their grateful passengers in the Haymarket bus station.

Below: *A helter-skelter greeted visitors to the Hoppings at one of the entrances to the Town Moor site, while caravans, trucks and canvas tents mark the outline of the huge oval ring in which all the fun of the fair was promised and reliably delivered. The scene is viewed from a tiny aircraft flying at 1500 ft (just three times the height of Blackpool Tower to you and me), making the excited fairground visitors look like ants on a driveway. The Town Moor covers an area of approximately 1000 acres, though the Hoppings never stood on more than 30 acres of it. The origins of the event can be traced back for over a century and the fair is claimed to be the largest non-permanent event of its type in the world. The photograph was taken in 1957.*

Right: *This late 1950s aerial view was seen from an altitude of just 2000 feet above the streets of Newcastle on a warm summer's afternoon. The plucky photographer was looking in the direction of the Tyne when he released his shutter as the light aircraft slowly droned across the clear blue sky. Several familiar landmarks are easily recognisable thanks to the picture's sharpness. St Thomas' Church stands at the top left corner beside the South African war memorial and a short walk away from Percy Street and the retail heart of the city. Nearer the camera a border of trees surrounds the Newcastle Playhouse, and to the right of this faithful servant the modern University of Newcastle complex dominates the area alongside Claremont Road.*

Courtesy of the Ward Philipson Collection

Courtesy of the Ward Philipson Collection

High days & holidays

Both pages: The Royal Agricultural Show was only held in Newcastle five times, and was to eventually find a permanent site in Warwickshire. It always attracted a huge number of visitors, and not just those interested in farming and agriculture! The Show, with its many fascinating displays to view, animals to interest the children, and bands to sit and listen to, made a great day out for the entire family. Preparations for the Show started well in advance of the big day as the stands were erected, displays set up, plant and machinery moved in, catering arranged, and a thousand and one other tasks dealt with. It was a mammoth task. The livestock was always popular among visitors to the Royal Show, who appear to have adopted uniform dress. The gabardine 'mac' was worn by the vast majority of the people in the crowd in the 1956 Show and the flat cap, of course, was obligatory wear for the men. This is the real working end of the Show, and the crowd's keen interest is apparent as one of Dales ponies is put through its paces.

Visitors of quite a different kind opted to view the equestrian events, and our second photograph would indicate that the Duke of Northumber-land - whose 'chuffed' smile says it all - was a prizewinner in one of the riding events *(below)*. The Duke would soon find himself the fortunate possessor of the silver trophy, temptingly displayed on the table in the foreground of the picture, to be presented to him by the Queen Mother, who had a genuine interest in the riding events. There were no spare seats in the stand that day, and one or two people in the crowd have their cameras ready to record the prizegiving ceremony. The displays of fruit, flowers and vegetables were not to be missed, and the Queen Mum appears to have enjoyed her conducted tour of the prizewinning entries *(bottom)*. This display of produce entered by the Durham County branch of the NFU ingeniously mixes shiny apples, well scrubbed turnips and magnificent blooms to startling effect. This is one photograph we would have enjoyed seeing in colour!

Both pages: *Blaydon Races Fever hit Newcastle in 1962 when the centenary of the well known races, kept alive in the world-famous song, was celebrated with week-long revelries. The great occasion produced a carnival atmosphere across the entire city, and events of every kind were arranged, from Old Time Music Hall, held in the Black Bull in Blaydon, to ballroom dancing in a marquee in the Exhibition Park. An old horse-drawn omnibus was re-introduced to the streets of Newcastle during the week before the big day. How many readers remember being driven around the city centre as they sampled the public transport of for-mer days? One shilling for adults and six-pence for children was the price charged (five and two-and-a-half new pence respectively), and the old bus was a great hit with the general public. The bus took part in the grand procession along Scotswood Road on 4th June (far right), though it is not evident in our photograph. That was a day to remember - as those who were there will know! Traffic in the city was almost at a standstill, and the Centenary Queen, 25-year-old Sheila McFarlane, almost missed her coronation, to the consternation of the officials! After the delayed crowning ceremony came the various events: a vintage car rally from Blaydon to Newcastle; a long distance cycle race; brass band music in Exhibition Park; a concert in Eldon Square given by the Band of the Coldstream Guards, and much, much more.*
The last of the Blaydon Races were run on 2nd September 1916, and the riots caused by that day's events have become *part of our history. The favourite, Anxious Moments, won by an easy 10 lengths - but when the jockey weighed in after the race the horse was found to be carrying a stone less than it should have been. The swindle having been discov-ered, Anxious Moments was disqualified. Naturally enough those pitmen and workers who had placed legitimate bets were more than slightly annoyed when they lost all their money. The angry crowd stormed the weighing room and stewards room and set it on fire; they knocked down the bookmakers' stalls - and threw every jockey they could find in the river. Stewards hastily declared the entire race void - which in turn infuriated the backers of Jeanie, who had come in second! In a further decision the stewards returned all the stakes - but the riot spelled the end for Blaydon Races.*

Both pages: The Town Moor Hoppings has an atmosphere of its very own that has to be experienced to be appreciated. The whirr and hum of the rides, the loud beat of the music, several different tunes fighting with each other for attention, the shouts of the man who bravely volunteers to guess your weight, and the squeals of the girls as they rise to the top of the big wheel. And the food! The toffee apples, dark red and shining as if they have been varnished, the paper bags of crunchy brandy snap and the ice cream, in tubs, cornets or wafers, and the shocking pink candy floss. Remember the time when it was sold from booths where it was spun around a stick while you waited? The sterile, pre-bagged confection we buy today bears little resemblance to the real thing - after all, sticky fingers were all part of the day's fun! The annual Hoppings is possibly the largest non-permanent fair in the world, and its hundreds of amusements, rides and stalls cover around 30 acres. In days gone by, of course, the rides were all steam driven, from the merry-go-rounds to the swing boats which closely resembled the Riverboat, pictured in June

1961 *(left).* A very scary ride, this, especially for those sitting on the outer limits of the ride. The swing boat ended up almost vertical, and with no safety belts in place it was a case of hanging on like grim death if you didn't want to end up as part of the accident statistics! The Hoppings is a much looked-forward-to event, and by the end of every April excitement is already building up, especially among the younger members of the family. Everyone hopes, of course, for good weather - and the prayed-for sunshine doesn't always materialise, as our photograph from 1968 shows *(below centre)!* In mud such as this, the real answer is a pair of stout wellies, but what teenage girl wants to be seen wearing uncool rubber boots? Since the 1960s the rides at the Hoppings have become progressively more sophisticated; contrast the 127ft Liberty Wheel which visited the Hoppings for the first time in 1995 with the big wheel of former days! It's after dark, of course, that the huge fairground looks its best. The usual huge crowds turned up in June 1971 *(bottom),* and our scene shows some of the wonder and excitement revealed in the faces of the visitors, and the glow of the hundreds of coloured lights against the night sky. That was the year the site fees were increased and the Fair opened on Friday evening as a bonus. The history of the annual Hoppings goes back to 1882, when the event was a Temperance Festival with children's games, sport and music. It has come a long way since then! By the mid 1990s visitors parked more than 22,000 cars during the week of the Fair, which had more attractions than ever before.

Below centre: 'Richard II' is being performed at the Tyne Theatre and Opera House, and the actors, Jane Majeer, Jeremy Irons, Imogen Stubbs and Henry Goodman, smile for the camera in November 1986 in front of the historic theatre. Built in 1867, the theatre has had a chequered history. Enhanced by the latest in Victorian stage technology which included ropes, pulleys and gear wheels, it enjoyed runaway success in its earlier years, and in 1919 was closed for renovation. It reopened as the luxurious Stoll Picture Theatre with the film 'Tarzan of the Apes'. In 1929 the cinema was wired for sound - the wonder technology of the day, and hundreds of cinemagoers came to shed romantic tears over Jolson's rendering of 'Danny Boy' in 'The Singing Fool'. 'Danny Boy' was of course destined to become everyone's favourite song. The famous (and oft misquoted) line 'You ain't heard nothing yet' was spoken by Al Jolson in the film. Through the 60s and 70s the Stoll slid downhill into soft porn films, and closed in 1974. Three years later it reverted to its original use as a theatre and went on to produce only live shows.

Bottom: The 1920s were, for many, years of national depression and long-lasting unemployment; in fact in 1928 a national Unemployment Fund was created - the 'dole' of a pitiful sum that was scarcely enough to keep body and soul together. The Prince of Wales, who later became King Edward VIII, was well known for his interest in helping the unemployed, and when it was decided to hold an exhibition to demonstrate the continued strength of industry in the North East, the 'Society Prince' was the obvious choice of royal personage to open it. He opened the North East Coast Exhibition on 14th May 1929, and it proved a huge success with the four million plus people who visited it. There was much to see and experience: the Palace of Arts; the promenade and boating lake; and the exhibits and displays put on by local industries such as Vickers Armstrong, Swan Hunter and Andrews' Liver Salts. Our photograph shows the Empire Marketing Board Pavilion at the Exhibition; what a pity the rather elegant Art Deco building was demolished afterwards! The Prince of Wales became King in 1936, only to abdicate after 325 days in order to marry American divorcee Wallis Simpson.

Above: Judging by the eager crowd waiting for a ride, this miniature railway was an enormously popular attraction at the Tyneside Summer Exhibition staged in Exhibition Park in August 1968. The miniature train was a fascination not only to the children but to their parents as well, and if we take note of the occupants of the carriage we can see that it was not only the kiddies who were enjoying the thrill of the ride! Here the beautifully detailed locomotive huffs and puffs eagerly as its lucky driver prepares to take his next load of passengers on their exciting trip - though one or two of the smallest children look a little unsure about the hissing engine. What a wonderful job this driver had! The little train drew a host of fathers (and a few mothers), who no doubt envied the fortunate man who was lucky enough to have landed the job of driving this little beauty. Many enthusiasts would no doubt have been only too willing to part with cash from their own pockets for the privilege of driving this beautiful scaled-down loco!

Below: When Julian Herington opened the Flora Robson Playhouse on 11th September 1962, he dreamed of seeing the playhouse established in the same category as other famous repertory companies in Bristol, Birmingham and Liverpool. The building which had once been the Jesmond Playhouse was run down and dilapidated when the stagestruck young man decided to purchase and renovate it, and when no local builder was prepared to take on the work he rolled up his sleeves and got on with doing the job himself. The result was an elegant theatre with new dressing rooms, two bars, a restaurant and coffee bar, and an auditorium with plush seating for an audience of 643. Old street lamps became a special feature in the Lamp Room Grill. Dame Flora Robson gladly consented to the use of her name, and the Playhouse opened with Alexander Rivemale's 'Azouk'. Sadly, Herington's vision for the Flora Robson Playhouse never materialised and after struggling for many years, the theatre closed and was eventually demolished.

Wheels of time

Above: The usual stream of drivers searching for a parking space make their way down Grey Street in this busy scene from September 1962 - and if it came to a bet on their chances of success, most people would put their money on the little Mini! The Mini established itself as the car of the 60s, and its transverse engine made it possible to seat four passengers in comfort in spite of the car only being an incredible ten feet in length. The little vehicle was practical, affordable, fuel-efficient and easy to park - all features that helped to establish it as a firm favourite, especially with the student population and other hard-up younger drivers. The Royal Turks Head Hotel on the left of our photograph eventually closed and today belongs to Barclays. The hotel was RAC approved, and interestingly an entry in the RAC handbook for 1967 reveals that lunch at the three star establishment cost around 15/6d (77 pence in today's currency, if not in value), while an overnight stay in one of the hotel's 106 bedrooms with a good English breakfast the morning after would have set you back £3, which was reasonably expensive for the time.

Above right: The Newgate Street Co-op's Travel Bureau is featured in this scene from 1956. It was 'standing room only' at the counter, long before the introduction of comfy seats for the customers to view tempting package holidays displayed on computer screens. To be fair, the heyday of the package holiday had simply not arrived at the time this picture was taken, and the vast majority of holidays enjoyed by those who could afford them were at British seaside resorts. Air travel was generally reserved for film stars and VIPs and it would be another 10 years before ordinary people succumbed to the delights of Benidorm and Majorca. In the meantime, Newcastle's near-coastal location boosted the popularity of continental travel by sea to Europe and Scandinavia. By the late 1950s a growing number of local people could afford foreign travel, and, of course, many of their exciting expeditions would begin with a visit to the Co-op's Travel Bureau.

is the alarming ease with which the doors could be illegally opened and your precious car driven away by some young joyrider.... The car in front is the universally beloved Morris Minor, interestingly the first all-British car to sell more than one million. Developed by designer Alexander Issigonis, who also gave us the Mini, this tough little car has remained popular and is today attracting quite a following.

Top: Patient resignation is on the face of each of these would-be passengers queuing hopefully for their bus at the end of yet another working day. A hot meal will be waiting for some of them, and after that they could look forward to a couple of hours with their mates in the 'Dog and Duck'. If they were the type to enjoy the fireside rather than the tap room, it would be pipe and slippers time, with 'Crossroads', 'Take Your Pick' or perhaps 'Emergency Ward Ten' to watch on TV. This busy shot of the Worswick Street Bus Station is dated October 1962, the days when feminists had only just begun to burn their metaphoric bras, and there were still a large number of women who counted themselves as housewives. Their job was shopping, bringing up the children, cleaning the house, and making sure their man - who was the breadwinner - had a good meal every day. Scenes such as this were an everyday sight at Worswick Street; at the time around 150 buses left the Bus Station every hour.

Above: A constant stream of traffic makes its way into Newcastle from the Gateshead side of the Tyne Bridge, the arch of which can be made out in the right background. The photograph dates from the chilly month of February, 1975, and the cars in the shot are typical of the day. Many drivers still have a soft spot for the old Ford Anglia (well remembered for its distinctive rear window); the one in the left foreground bears a Northumberland registration. The Cortina Mk 1, identified by its 'ban the bomb' tail lights, is also worthy of a mention. The forerunner of the Mondeo and the Sierra, the Cortina was one of the first 'rep's express' cars, the object of every salesman's dream. Their drawback, as many Cortina owners found out to their cost,

Both pages: The Central Station is clad in a network of scaffolding as alterations are made to the portico in May 1959 *(below)*. The portico with which we are so familiar was a later addition to the station. Queen Victoria (who arrived, of course, by train) opened the Central Station in August 1850, and the portico, designed by Thomas Prosser, was added in 1863. The well known local architect John Dobson designed the station itself, and his trainshed, with its fluid spans of curved wrought ironwork was a work of art in anyone's book. Future years were to see many famous trains pulling into the station, with names such as 'The City of Newcastle', 'Flying Fox', 'The Flying Scotsman' and 'Silver Jubilee'. July 1927 saw hundreds of railway buffs and local officials greet 'Flying Fox' as it pulled into Central at 3.20pm, having left Kings Cross at 9.50am for the first non stop service between London and Newcastle.

The 'Diamond Crossing' approach to Newcastle Central was at one time the largest and the busiest railway crossing in the world, and our two views looking westwards into the station give us a hint of the amount and the variety of rail traffic it carried.

Our photograph from 1962 shows the 'Tyne Loop' electrified system *(bottom),* which was the basis of our present Metro - the Tyneside Rapid Transit System - the first section of which opened in 1981. During the early 1960s electric, diesel and steam trains all existed side by side, though diesel was to eventually dominate. The second view of the Diamond Crossing dates from 1959 *(far left);* compare the two photographs and spot the number of changes which took place during the three years which separated the shots.

Both pages: 'I'll meet you under the clock.' How often has this phrase been uttered by travellers down the years since the Central Station was first opened? The lakes of water on the concourse tell us that the clock had obviously had a narrow escape when these scenes were captured back in July 1961. The wooden cladding on John Dobson's magnificent vaulted ceiling has clearly been under threat; high pressure jets of water play on the roof as fire crews battle to save this important part of Newcastle's history, while water still cascades down from the roof in our dramatic photograph. The smoke charred walls and piles of rubble and debris within the station concourse tell us that it was a near thing, and crowds of would-be passengers gather together out of harm's way. This was not the first time fire had threatened the station, and nor would it be the last, the latest having been as recent as 1997. The Central Station is a marvel of Victorian engineering, combining artistic and graceful lines with practical use. Queen Victoria and Prince Albert visited Newcastle to declare the station - built at a cost of £100,000 - officially open on 29th August 1850. This was the Queen's second visit within a few months - only the previous year she had opened Robert Stephenson's High Level Bridge, across which trains approached Newcastle via the busy railway crossing, pictured here in 1961 *(above)*. On a different note, readers will spot the construction of Crudders Park tower blocks taking place in the background.

At the shops

Through all the changing scenes of life...people need to go shopping. And Northumberland Street has always had an overwhelming choice of stores since it was established as a major shopping street at the end of the 19th century. Accustomed as we are to seeing this part of Northumberland Street as a traffic free zone, it seems rather strange to look back to the days when buses and cars were seen here. This view dates from October 1986, and the pavements were crowded in this shoppers'

paradise. Woolworths, Fenwicks, Marks & Spencer, Littlewoods - the many department stores beckoned, each inviting passers by to part with their cash. John J Fenwick's first shop was at Number 5 Northumberland Street, where he sold mantles and furs in the days before the tide of public opinion swung violently against the wearing of fur. For many years, the fact that your collar was genuine was often reinforced with the head of the unfortunate animal. Mr Fenwick made the move to the store's present site in 1885.

Below: The pace of suburban life appeared more relaxed in 1956 when this scene was noticed and recorded by a photographer on West Road. In truth, the picture was probably taken to show people how stylish the Co-op supermarket looked, complete with smart curved entrance, concrete canopy and thoughtful clock to aid passing shoppers and motorists. The styling was very modern for its day and the simple, clean lines of the store contrast sharply with other 'corner shops' and the over-head trolley bus cables running along West Road. Our eyes are inevitably drawn to the people featured in the picture. Several women and at least four prams can be seen, passing the time of day with each other just before dinner time, catching up on the gossip and comparing notes on the progress made by their respective babies. Happy days.

Bottom: The Grainger Market has changed little over the years; this photograph dates from 1970 and the market was as popular then as now. The market has an atmosphere of its very own, the subtle scents of oranges and apples competing with the sharper odours of onions and leeks.... Traditionally, you could buy more than fruit and vegetables at the Grainger Market. Most of the things needed by the average household could be found beneath its elegant arches, whether you were looking for fresh flowers or a shoulder of lamb for your Sunday lunch. The market hall had (and still has) a cheerful and bustling atmosphere, and stalls such as the one on the far right were a riot of colour, with its containers of daffodils and tulips (or roses and chrysanthemums, according to the time of year). The market hall was designed back in the 19th century by Grainger and Dobson, and opened in 1835. Today the Grainger Market is a Grade I listed building and is a magnet for tourists; its Marks & Spencer Penny Bazaar is an obvious attraction.

Both pages: *These well-stocked fruit stalls in the Bigg Market would have made a good starting place for a lot of Newcastle house-wives, who week after week would catch a bus into town and tour the markets to find the best - and cheapest - apples, pears, oranges, grapefruit and bananas. Buying potatoes and tomatoes from one stall, apples and sprouts from another and perhaps cabbage and a couple of grapefruit from a third have always been part of the fun of bargain hunting in the market (below). The prices charged by markets and street traders have traditionally been a few coppers cheaper than the average high street greengrocer would charge, and a weekly walk around the market stalls could save a shilling or two here and there, and stretch the*

inadequate housekeeping money a little bit further. The Bigg Market, whose name refers to barley rather than size (which they say doesn't matter), is nevertheless a little gem. It is the city's oldest market, and dates back to Norman times. Our pigeon's eye view of the Bigg Market gives us a wider perspective, and the nostalgic view, captured before the old Town Hall was demolished and replaced by a modern office block, will revive many memories (left). Spot the back entrance to Bainbridges, where a sun blind has been pulled down to protect the goods on display. Emerson Muschamp Bainbridge opened his famous store in Newcastle in 1837 - the first department store in the whole of Europe. By 1887 the store had a staff of more than 400.

This page: Unfortunately we have no date for either of our two views of the Quayside Market, though boats were still being moored on the riverside, which was obviously still a working jetty at the time.

A Sunday Market has been held here for hundreds of years - the city's Historical Records refer to it as far back as 1736, and it was probably in existence long before then. Three of Newcastle's famous bridges make a stunning background to the view as hundreds of punters browse among the stalls hoping to pick up a bargain. The children, of course, have their eye on the helium filled balloons which still have as much pull today as they did when a photographer captured this charming view *(bottom)*. The crowds were even greater in our earlier photograph, and a number of slick-talking salesmen have set up their stalls hoping to make themselves a few bob, though frustratingly we can't quite make out exactly what they were selling! Whatever it was, the salesmen's patter was obviously entirely riveting, as many eyes in the crowd are directed on the demonstration, while the photographer and his (or her) camera goes largely unnoticed. Interestingly, men both old and young are in the majority in this group, though a few ladies can be seen on the outskirts of the

action. The preponderance of males makes it unlikely that the subject of the presentation has anything to do with domestic arrangements or fashion. Could this fast-talking trader perhaps be demonstrating an ingenious invention for removing condensation from windows or pet hairs from furniture? Slick-talking salesmen have always been around to charm the pennies and shillings from people's pockets, and whatever was on offer that day, a few pound notes or even fivers were no doubt handed over by punters eager to part with their cash.

Earning a crust

Above: This scene of dedicated activity and efficiency was recorded in April 1961 when the new district traffic control for Newcastle Central Station was introduced. At the time, the new facility was the last word in modern technology, from the individual panels mapping the railway network conveniently placed in front of each operator to the telephone system which kept the lines of communication open. The march of technology, however, never ceases and eventually further developments made this traffic control system redundant. Interestingly, the panels, along with the signalling system, were preserved and are today lodged in the George Stephenson workshop. English Heritage hope to restore the old equipment, which after all is part of Newcastle's rich railway history, to its original order. George Stephenson, the father of the modern locomotive, was only 14 when, working with his father in a coal mine, he first developed his interest in mining machines and steam engines. He set up his own factory in Newcastle in 1823, building locomotives.

It's a long way mining from Utah to Gateshead

From the 19th century through to the present day the history of the world wide mining industry has been marked by expansion, development and innovation. One company which has travelled along that path rising from modest beginnings as a scrap metal business into a multi-national organisation catering to the mining industry is Gateshead's EIMCO.

Despite the decline of the mining industry in the North East of England and throughout the whole of the United Kingdom some mining-dependent companies in the North are still thriving after adapting their trade to fit the changing economic climate. That description includes the Team Valley's Eimco. The company specialises in the refurbishment and redesign of used Eimco mining production equipment.

Equipment of this type operates in very rugged underground mining conditions and is often received for repair in a very poor state - which is where the company comes into its own. The machinery is rebuilt to an 'as new' specification and covered by a comprehensive warranty.

When many mines were closed much of their spare equipment was thrown out: in response the company set up a system to whereby it could repair and update discarded or worn out underground diesel equipment. The company will flame-proof underground diesel machinery to stringent European standards, create new power systems which ensure that they need less maintenance than previously and in addition ergonomically redesign machines - in effect the equipment is remanufactured.

Flame-proof equipment is prepared at the Team Valley site whilst specialist equipment such as FLP Diesel Power packs are tested at Eimco's own Dynamometer test facility. Equipment taken in for this treatment includes heavy load carriers, roof support trailers and miners. These are usually soft rock (coal, gypsum and potash) mining plant and machinery.

Although the company only appeared in the Newcastle area in the 1950s Eimco's roots go back to 1892, to a small business founded in Salt Lake City, Utah, in the USA. The following three decades saw major growth for mining and smelting in the American inter-mountain state of Utah, not least as a result of the Great War of 1914-18; Eimco was at the forefront in both mine working and smelting.

Below: *EIMCO offices in Salt Lake City, Utah, USA in the early part of the 20th century.*

were then on supply to the British mining industry on lend-lease terms. By the end of the second world war setting up a UK operation was considered to be worthwhile by the company both to service Eimco's machines already in use in British mines and also to meet future market requirements.

In May 1948 Eimco (GB) Ltd was formed and local manufacture began with the new company's headquarters in Leeds. Growth followed from sales to the NCB and development drivages and development programmes. In the post war building boom sales were also made to contractors involved in such operations as hydro-electric schemes for the north of Scotland, the Woodhead tunnel and many other civil engineering contracts.

By the late 1920s the firm had moved progressively into mining equipment, refurbishing used machinery, and rapidly establishing for itself a reputation for rugged, reliable products. Sales quickly expanded beyond the USA and into Europe.

In 1931 Eimco took the first step towards industry leadership by creating a fully-fledged engineering department. Innovation quickly became a byword as the company began designing its own equipment. A significant early development was the Eimco Findlay loader, a pioneering machine to help hardrock and metal miners make the switch from hand labour to mechanisation. That compressed-air Rockershovel invented by Findlay and Royle for Eimco in 1931 is even now, regardless of the actual manufacturer, still widely known as an 'EIMCO'.

The development of that unique early underground loader proved vitally important for Eimco's growth. The Findlay loader or Rockershovel dramatically altered the way hardrock mining was conducted and established the young company as a world leader in the supply and manufacture of proven and innovative machinery. Before and throughout the 1939-45 war the Eimco Corporation was represented in the UK by its agents Ingersoll Rand. A considerable number of machines

Leadership in loader development soon extended into Eimco's Load Haul Dump Line the first in North America and subsequently across the world. Side Dump Loaders were developed by the company in Britain. These units and their add-on options made the side dump loader one of the most versatile underground machines ever manufactured followed later by the Free Steered Vehicle.

*Top: EIMCO's Gateshead offices. **Above left:** EIMCO dump-truck on road test. **Below:** EIMCO 850 operations on the Doncaster Bypass construction, circa 1960.*

In 1952 another division of Eimco was formed in the UK to manufacture filters. A manufacturing plant capable of handling large fabrications was needed and two years later the present Eimco factory in the Team Valley Estate at Gateshead began operation. For a time additional bays at the factory coped with increasing requirements until increasing demand for both the filters and the mining machinery made it necessary to have even larger factories for both divisions. The Filter Division then moved into a separate factory in St Neots whilst the remaining Mining Division occupied the whole premises at Team Valley continuing to expand to include a large new facility.

After pioneering mine mechanisation in the USA with the rocker shovel in 1931 innovations continued in the UK. In 1952 the firm's famous 621 rocker-shovel was developed. This was the first crawler-mounted over-shot loader and subsequently it led to the development of both the 622 and, in the USA the 630, rocker shovel. Eimco developed the comprehensive range of 600 series crawler-mounted Electro/hydraulic side dump loader machines including the very popular 612, 625 and 627 loaders. More than 2,000 of those loaders were eventually to be sold in the UK, Canada, Mexico, Turkey, Poland, Hungary, Spain Egypt, China, India, Vietnam and Japan.

Top: *EIMCO Low Profile Dumper.* ***Right:*** *EIMCO 622 Rockershovel loading in a coal mine.*

In 1978 the company opened a new 70,000 sq ft factory at Gateshead giving it a total of 140,000 sq ft on the site which in total covered more than 360,000 sq ft. The investment including plant and machinery in that year cost £4 million.

In addition to its main offices and factory complex at Gateshead Eimco also had offices in Paris, and in Madrid and Oviedo in Spain. These offices provided back-up throughout East and West Europe and North Africa.

Eimco continued expanding its role as one of the world's foremost underground mining machinery suppliers through several acquisitions during the 1970s and 1980s. The equipment obtained from these acquisitions included continuous miners scoops, load haul dumps, roof bolters, drill jumbos, shuttle cars and rail transportation vehicles.

By 1970 the company was part of the Envirotech Mining Machinery Group still based in Salt Lake City but by the 1980s Eimco had became a division of Baker Hughes Mining a British company with other fully independent divisions operating in the United Kingdom, all of whom were involved in supplying the energy industries.

In 1989 the company became part of Tamrock, a company with headquarters in Tampere, Finland.

In 1987 the company had been employing some 300 people but by the late 1990s, largely as result of the decline of the British coal industry only some 36 multi-

skilled engineers and administrators remained on the site at Team Valley - 1996 was the first year for a decade in which the firm had announced no redundancies. Fortunately for the future of the company, whilst mining may have been in decline in Britain, in the rest of the world the mining industries were booming.

Today Eimco supplies markets in China, Poland, Russia and South Africa whilst its main UK customer is RJB Mining.

Products continue to be specialist machines for loading and transport underground built to flame-proof requirements. Eimco's main sales comprise its equipment with flame-proof diesel engines, carrying capacities of up to 40 tonnes on relatively small size machines which are flexible, safe and versatile. The firm's technical superiority in its field particularly the high carrying capacity of its equipment and the flame-proof systems which have been approved by authorities around the world has ensured that Eimco has become the largest supplier of this type of mining machinery in Britain.

Amongst Eimco's current range are tracked loaders and rubber tyred vehicles for the loading and transport of both material and people. The range of machines almost without exception includes a significant hydraulic content and is powered either by electric motors, diesel engine or battery in each case flame-proofed to comply with relevant legislation and standards. Plans for the future include smaller, very flexible vehicles and the development of a high capacity 35 tonne coal hauler.

Today Eimco (Great Britain) Ltd is a Sandvik company and part of VA-EIMCO with headquarters in Zeltweg, Austria. The company is internationally renowned for the manufacture of equipment associated everywhere in the world with the development and transport of underground coal.

The company's business philosophy is simple: 'to develop and continue to supply unique cost saving, loading and transporting equipment to the mining industry'. It is surely not a philosophy that the company's founders all those years ago in Utah would have found much to disagree with.

Top left: EIMCO 850 Dump Truck. *Below:* EIMCO plant, Gateshead.

Above: This shot of Eldon Square as it was will take many of our readers on a trip down Memory Lane. The date was 29th May 1962; many changes had already been made in Newcastle and many more changes were yet to come. The line of properties on the right of our photograph are all that survived the red pen of the planners, and their use has changed from business premises to the speciality clothes shops and bistros that we know today. Where at the time of the photograph we could arrange our insurance cover at the British Oak we can now sit and contemplate the changing city over a cappuccino and a pastry at Boskoff's Coffee Shop. The original elegant three sided square was largely the work of the talented Richard Grainger, who constructed all but four of the properties in the 1820s. Eldon Square was, in the fulness of time, to lend its name to our 'new' 10-acre shopping centre, which was opened in 1976. Since then the facility has wormed its way into the affections of the shopping public, and we can scarcely imagine Newcastle without it.

Above right: What motorist has not at some time gone through the frustration of hunting through all his pockets (or her purse!) for change, only to come up with bits and pieces which the machine is not built to accept? Depending on the viewpoint, parking meters became either the bane or the blessing of our lives! Our photograph is from February 1970, and Judith Barklay demonstrates the use of the machines, which we suppose to have been newly introduced to Newcastle, though Britain saw the first parking meters as long ago as 1958. Though the country adopted decimal currency in 1971, the first of the new decimal coins were actually introduced in 1968, and for some time the old shilling and the new five pence coin existed side by side with equal value. There were widespread fears that shops would use the changeover to increase their prices - in the event, fears that were not unfounded! In the beginning, the idea of decimal coinage was very unpopular, but very soon people were swayed by the ease of working in tens rather than in twelves and twenties! In due course metrication became the issue and the outcome was inevitable; the country would have to go metric - every inch of the way....

From spiders' webs to websites

Many readers will have seen vehicles carrying the name James Atkinson and wondered exactly who James Atkinson might be.

Today James Atkinson and Co Ltd is part of Metano International Holdings and is a major supplier of road tanker fittings and containers.

The firm's founder, James Atkinson, an orphan, was educated at Ackworth Quaker School in Pontefract where he lived with foster parents.

During the second world war James Atkinson worked in engineering in Newcastle. In 1945 he took advantage of a government set-up scheme and along with a partner, Ernie Tibbles, founded the firm of Atkinson and Tibbles, an instrument-making and repair business servicing such equipment as cameras, theodolites and levels and James set up his own firm in 1946.

The business was located in Newcastle beneath the railway arches on the Gateshead side of the High Level Bridge. Expanding into pattern making 'Atkinsons' occupied all three floors of the premises.

Ian Harland, the firm's present owner, recalls that when he was young he considered 'Uncle Jimmy' to be 'somewhat eccentric'.

James Atkinson would visit their house in Darras Hall and, much to Ian's mother's embarrassment, if he saw a spider he would quickly pull out an empty match box and put the spider in it. Why? Because spiders' webs make excellent cross hairs in surveying instruments. The unlucky spider would then be released in the factory to accompany thousands of others making raw materials for the firm.

Visiting the factory was a source of fascination for Ian as a young boy. The roof was low and the lights were wrinkled glass shades with clear bulbs. For at least 18 inches from the ceiling down was nothing but a mat of spiders' webs.

Above: *James Atkinson.* **Below:** *A photograph of the Machine Shop taken in 1965.*

God help any fly entering there!! It was a simple matter to select the next cross-hair. Just lift up your arm and you had a handful of them.

The business did well. Casting patterns were needed throughout the north east for companies like Ingersoll Rand and Precision Products in Alston. Atkinsons' reputation culminated in an order from the City of New York to make patterns for light bulbs in the shape of fruit - apples, oranges, plums - for an exhibition. There were failures though too: a bottle washing plant built by Atkinsons for the Royal Infirmary in Newcastle was a small disaster when the hospital forget to tell the firm that not all the bottles would be the same size!

Evidence that the business was going well came in 1955 when James Atkinson walked into Rossleighs Garage to enquire about a car in the showroom - a shiny new Jaguar XK140. 'How much is that?' he asked standing in his scruffy brown overalls with his glasses perched in their usual place on his forehead '£1250' came the salesman's reply. 'I'll take it' James replied '- but I don't want the radio'. The rather posh salesman somewhat taken aback insisted 'you can't remove the radio from a car of this quality'. James Atkinson was adamant - he didn't want a radio and left the premises. Not liking to argue James went instead to find a friend who worked for another garage and asked him to go and buy the Jaguar - minus its radio - for him. Further negotiations took place at Rossleighs.

The salesman said 'Oh no, not again - what have you got against the radio anyway?' After some bartering however the car was secured, still with the radio, but with the price reduced by its value. James was ecstatic to have got the beautiful new car - but he never used the radio.

In 1969 the firm moved to a new 500 sq ft factory at Ellison Road in Dunston. Pattern making had become the main business and the firm had 20 employees. James' Jaguar was the first item to be put in the new factory because it needed some minor work doing to it

Above: *Export work - rear door for road tankers.*
Top: *Alan Young (a real engineer) at work in the Machine Shop. Alan, one of the firm's expert older generation, has now retired.*

This picture: *Part of the firm's ongoing programme of tests - the crash test of one of its containers on the French railways in the early 1990s.*

ATTENTION DANGER

RALENTISSEZ

ESSAI DE CONTAINER

A logistics error however meant that the machines were moved in before the car could move out - so here it had to stay for the next ten years. The car is still with the family!

Instruments continued to play an important role in the business. Having become a 20 per cent shareholder Dick Lindsley's particular skill was in the manufacture of specialised instruments. The British Standards Institute commissioned several instruments for testing the stickiness of sticky paper and Davy McKee commissioned a number of depth gauges for use on top of steel furnaces for measuring the level of molten metal inside the furnace. Several of those instruments went to the Kwang Yang steel works in Korea.

Not everything went smoothly however, on one occasion Northern Goldsmiths commissioned a display cabinet for rings and watches. James got his sums wrong on the reduction gearing and on initial tests the rings and watches were thrown everywhere. The cabinet is apparently still at Northern Goldsmiths but it is not switched on! Those who knew James Atkinson got used to his ways: he became an active Rotarian and would dress up for the Rotary meetings; his fellow Rotarians may however have been surprised to see him turn up one day apparently painted in camouflage. On that particular day he had bought some cheap paint and decided to mix it with a pillar-drill; just like the Goldsmiths' display cabinet the speed was wrong and James had to attend his Rotary meeting splattered with green paint.

In 1979 James Atkinson died and business began to fall away. Traditional surveying instruments were being replaced by lasers and different casting methods were being developed. Between 1979 and 1991 Atkinsons gradually declined to just one employee and faced almost certain closure.

In 1991 Ian Harland, whose father Stewart was James Atkinson's nephew, decided to buy the remaining business from the shareholders and turn it into a manufacturer of stainless steel fittings for the road tanker industry. John Wigham who had served his time at Atkinsons some years before was the first of the new employees and stainless steel manufacture was soon begun. Starting with Melton Tankers in Dewsbury Atkinson customers soon included Crane Fruehauf, Thompsons Tankers, the Milk Marketing Board and Feldbender in Germany. Manufacture of a milk tanker vent-valve for which Atkinsons held the patent was an excellent niche product which is still made today.

Seeing an opportunity to develop small pressure-vessels a number of units were made and, through what is now the sister company Metano, were rented to industry. The rental fleet grew at an extraordinary rate and Atkinsons grew along with Metano. Atkinsons developed a new role in support of the Metano rental fleet in cleaning' storage and management. Metano and Atkinsons won a contract with International Paint to provide reusable packages (IBCs - Intermediate Bulk Containers) for their paint products which includes a full service of cleaning, testing, repair and management of their logistics done by Atkinsons as well as the rental of the IBCs from Metano.

The company now operates from a two acre site at Rowlands Gill and today, happily for spiders, it no longer has any use for cobwebs!

World class engineering from BEL

Few Newcastle residents can fail to have noticed the BEL engineering works in St Peter's in Newcastle.

British Engines Limited (BEL), and the group of companies which now operates under its umbrella, started life on the same site in 1922 when the present Chairman's father and uncle first formed the company. Despite phenomenal growth in the subsequent decades the firm remains privately owned and it is proud to say that this ownership is still with the Lamb family - something of an achievement in these days of acquisitions, buy-outs and receiverships.

In 1922 when the two brothers from Glasgow - Harold T Lamb and Charles J Lamb - set up in business they could have had no idea what their venture would eventually lead to. The two brothers had a capital of only £7,500 and with just two men on their payroll and three machine tools between them they opened up for business as engineers. The fledgling firm began by repairing and reconditioning internal combustion engines from both ships and land-based applications along with a small amount of sub-contract machine work. In those early days both brothers worked at the benches and machines alongside their employees.

The old BEL site was somewhat different to that which exists to day: it was a single storey building of corrugated iron and could house fewer than twelve people. The firm has never moved from the site it still occupies though today the land and buildings take up some sixteen acres

with other small businesses operating in the peripheral areas immediately outside Newcastle.

In the early days the Lamb brothers found it extremely difficult to make ends meet. On one occasion a visiting Town Moor Fairground man brought a mechanical part to the company for repair but left before he had paid the bill. Harold Lamb bided his time and personally presented the bill to the man the following year when the fair returned to town! At times there was insufficient money in the cash box to pay the work force: when that happened the company secretary would get on his old bicycle and go round collecting money owed to the firm in order to have enough cash to make up the wages for the week.

Despite those early problems work began to mushroom. The years prior to the second world war were dominated by sub-contract machine work and the progressive entry into marine engineering in which engines from fishing vessels and fleet auxiliary boats coming into the River Tyne were serviced, overhauled or reconditioned.

The war years brought work from notable organisations such as DeHaviland, Rolls Royce and the Ministry of War (later Defence). That work entailed quality and precision as the vast majority of output found its way into aircraft including making parts for the first jet engine commercial airliner, the Comet. The company's efforts were rewarded by the continuing flow of such work for many years after 1945.

Below: *A section of the machine shop, 1959.*

his energies on developing their engineering business. As with any company reliant on sub-contract work BEL was subject to fluctuating business activity and as such seldom felt in control of its own destiny. The quest for product development began!

Cable terminating glands became part of BEL's product range in 1959 and ever since have been progressively designed, developed and manufactured into an internationally known range of products distributed via the company's CMP Products Division. CMP is now one of the world leaders in the field of cable glands and related accessories with offices in the USA, Dubai and Singapore.

BEL Valves was founded in the 1960s and was originally set up to produce high pressure valves for the chemical industry. During the oil boom of the 1970s and the exploitation of the North Sea oil fields the division began to supply valves to the offshore industry. It currently accounts for 45 per cent of company turnover and employs 50 per cent of the group's net assets. The main activity of BEL Valves is the manufacture of bespoke specialist valves, actuators and controls predominantly for the oil and gas fields. Primary markets served by the division are in the UK and Norwegian sectors of the North Sea. The BEL Valves division also has subsidiaries in the USA and Norway.

In addition to maintaining an interest in the business Charles J Lamb went into farming in the 1940s and had one of the leading herds of pedigree Ayrshire cattle at his farm in Morpeth. Engineering and mechanical equipment can however have seldom been far from his mind: an examination of his papers from the early 1950s shows a remarkable level of investment in agricultural hardware such as tractors, drills, electric fencing, petrol pumps, hydraulic trailers and elevators. Meanwhile brother Harold continued to concentrate all

Above left: H T Lamb pouring the first casting in the new Foundry, 1964. **Top:** *A view of the Milling Section, 1959.*

The first new member of the family to join the firm after 37 years of existence was Harold Lamb's son Graham who joined the company in 1959, having served an apprenticeship at Vickers Armstrong in Scotswood Road, Newcastle upon Tyne. Graham Lamb had also undergone training at DeHaviland Propellors.

During the late 1920s the company had started a small foundry producing components in a wide variety of non-ferrous alloys for the growing machine shop which by then was specialising in a select field of engineering, particularly sub-assemblies for general engineering purposes and for mining equipment. That latter activity grew into a considerable business in itself supplying plugs, sockets and cable couplers to, the then, British Coal.

In 1959 the company began using a new shell foundry process, organised from start to finish on a flow production basis, processing in a continuous run, from shell core and mould making at one end to melting, closing and pouring in the middle and knock-out fettling and despatch at the end. The company moved into a new foundry building in 1964, the new building being situated on Walker Road and Glasshouse Street near to

the firm's beginnings. The new facilities enabled the company to produce up to 250,000 shell castings each month weighing from a quarter of an ounce up to 40 lbs each and to great accuracy. The then new foundry and office block added 60,000 square feet to the company's premises giving a total working area of 175,000 square feet and providing ample room for the £300,000 worth of new equipment the company was able to buy that year.

Top: *General view of the old Foundry, 1952.*
Above: *An early NC Machine, 1975.*

The business certainly needed the extra space, business was booming. Nineteen sixty-two had seen for the first time the manufacture of high pressure valves and associated fittings for the petro-chemical industry. Producing a wide range of valves to customer specification, these products were traded under BEL Valves which was and is one of the very few organisations capable of designing, manufacturing and testing valves in specialised alloy steels up to 100,000 lbs PSI. These valves are sold throughout the world for petro-chemical and oil/gas applications both on-shore and subsea.

Virtually in parallel with its valves development the company was entering the field of hydraulics in the form of an axial piston pump. Production of pumps of varying capacities was made easier by further investment, not least by the acquisition of a Reynolds motor in 1987 and a Sauer Sundstrand motor which was purchased in 1989. Both of these motors together with the wide range of pumps are designed, manufactured and tested within the firm's Rotary Power Division and are distributed to an international market. Currently the Rotary Power division's main activities include the design, development and manufacture of high quality piston pumps and motors for the mining, subsea, offshore, steel, chemical and construction industries in addition to the manufacture of rotary-percussive rock-drill heads for Boart(UK) Ltd a joint venture between BEL and Boart. The division operates on the international market and has two wholly owned subsidiaries in the USA and Germany.

Other developments over the years included mining equipment, air drills, roto-lift, chain hoists and many other light to medium-sized engineering products which give the company a diverse product portfolio within most major engineering-producing industries.

A further development in recent years is Stadium Packing Services which makes boxes on behalf of many large companies. The Stadium Packing division provides a comprehensive packing, inspection and preservation service to industry in the Northeast of England and Scotland and is based on sites in Gateshead and Glasgow.

Above: *The old Pattern Shop, 1950.*
Below: *The old Shell Foundry, 1950.*

Another business acquisition is BARIC Systems - a unit providing Lubrication and Seal Oil systems designed, built and distributed worldwide. Baric Systems was originally formed in 1968 and was acquired by BEL in 1997. Baric Systems is recognised as a leading manufacturer of dry gas seal systems, API systems, hydraulic and pneumatic control panels, hydraulic power systems and API lube, seal oil systems.

The various divisions which make up the BEL group are themselves serviced by an up-to-date Administration and Services Division.

Strategically the company operates as ten independent business units which are each responsible for their own sales, manufacturing and profitability via dedicated personnel: BEL Valves manufacturing globe, gate and check valves up to 40 inches in diameter; Rotary Power making pumps, motors and rock drills; CMP Products making brass and aluminium cable glands-couplers; the BEL Foundry making ferrous, non-ferrous and stainless steel castings for BEL and external customers; BEL Grapnel producing equipment for retrieval of sub sea anchorage; Belmach machine tool agents; BW

Engineering sub-contract machining work; Stadium Packing Services box making and storage; Baric Systems lube and seal oil systems and lastly Controls - valve actuator and control systems.

The most recently acquired division of the BEL group is the Stephenson Gobin company acquired in 2000. The Stephenson Gobin engineering base is located in Bishop Auckland.

Above: *Latest addition - Scharmann Horizontal Borer, 1965.* **Top:** *Company vehicles lined up outside the premises on Glasshouse Street, Newcastle in 1954.*

quality products at competitive prices - BEL looks forward to continued managed growth.

The company is still in the hands of the Lamb family. Graham Lamb's is chairman, Sheila Longo (Charles Lambs' daughter) is a non-executive director. Of Graham's four sons, two - Alexander and Nicholas - joined the business. Alexander Lamb a Chartered Accountant is active, being a Director within the

This latest company specialises in the field of fire safety systems, power transmission, designing and producing a wide range of electromagnetic clutches and brakes, power supplies, gearboxes, geared motors and solenoids.

BEL currently employs 700 people mainly in Newcastle where it occupies a production facility of 500,000 square feet. Although predominantly operating from its St Peter's site the company also has small units in Killingworth, Gateshead, Glasgow, Germany, Norway, Singapore, Dubai, Texas and Ohio in the USA - in addition to an international agency and distribution network.

To ensure the company maintains its leading market position people-development is at the forefront of the company's objectives ensuring that individuals maximise their own potential and career aspirations in tandem with the company's business requirements. In 1966 the company commitment to training was clearly illustrated by the capital investment directed towards the creation of an off-the-job Training Centre dedicated to craft/technical apprenticeships and adult skill upgrading. This invaluable centre still operates within the St Peter's site, and produces engineering craftsmen from amongst whom the company ultimately gains its technicians, supervisors and managers.

In conjunction with its Positive Human Resource Policy the company has achieved three Investors in People Awards: the first in 1993 renewed in 1996 and, following a full review, again in 1999.

With the dedication of experienced personnel and continual investment in plant and machinery - which allows the firm to develop and market its

Group. Nicholas Lamb is based in Glasgow and is part of the firm's packaging business there. Shirley Wilson (Harold Lamb's daughter) had three children the eldest of whom, Andrew, was tragically killed in a motor car accident in 1991 at the age of only 36 and who up until then had been taking a very active role in the company. Shirley's other son, David, is now also in the business taking an active role in Stephenson Gobin as well as being a director of BEL. As for the founders, Harold T Lamb died in June 1970 six weeks after the death of his wife and Charles J Lamb died in March 1986.

Today the company has a multiplicity of businesses producing their sophisticated products on state-of-the-art machine tools including solid modelling CAD and FE Analysis. The engineering facility is the largest in the north of England and BEL is probably the largest privately owned engineering company left in the region. With an annual turnover of around £55 million the original investment of £7,500 by the Lamb brothers has produced an extraordinary return in exchange for their hard work and initiative.

Right:*The present Chairman, Harold Graham Lamb.*
Top: *Wickman Section, 1965.*

Go North East: leading the way

There can be no reader who has not at one time or another used public transport and in particular used the region's bus services. Buses can be an extraordinarily source of nostalgia. How many times have we spent on buses breathlessly travelling to the cinema to meet a date, taking the hospital bus to visit a sick relative or a new mother, just going shopping or travelling to work? How many of us have raced up the stairs to occupy our favourite seat? How many of us sampled our first illicit cigarette on the top deck or stole our first kiss on the back seat of a bus? And how many of us risked our lives jumping on or off the open platform in our youth? It takes you back doesn't it?

The story of bus services in Newcastle and its neighbourhood is a long one and one of the current operating companies, Go North East, can trace its ancestry back through many decades. The Go North East bus company's origins can be traced back to

tramcars in the closing years of 19th century. In 1896 a national group of companies was founded called British Electric Traction (BET); that concern soon established operations nationwide. Pre-existing tramways at Tynemouth and Gateshead, both dating back to 1883, were bought by BET followed by further expansion in the area. The Northern General Transport Co Ltd was created in November 1913 as a holding company for those operations under the BET umbrella.

Many older readers will remember trams, but the battle between bus and tram began very early. The opening salvo in that war was fired soon after 'Northern's creation when Gateshead's first bus company, which had also started in 1913, was transferred to Northern.

Above: Bristol VRT 3380 in yellow livery crosses the Tyne Bridge. Below: Leyland Leopard 2537, one of a large number purchased in the late 60s, a Manors Station.

The first bus ran from Low Fell to Chester-le-Street. After the first world war Northern's activities mushroomed. It would take until 1951 however before the last tram would be seen in Gateshead but all the while buses inexorably chipped away at their routes with Northern going further and faster than many of its competitors.

Northern General Transport had works in Bensham where it built its own bus bodies. In 1933 Northern started building its own buses in their entirety. With low railway bridges in the area the company needed the best engineering and the largest capacity a single-decker could deliver. The solution to the company's problem was undertaking the job itself. Those unique vehicles, made in large numbers, marked Northern out for the next two decades. A remaining example of one is now kept for the benefit of posterity by the Northern Omnibus Trust.

A culture of vehicle innovation would become a tradition at Northern but in the meantime a threat appeared. In the late 1940s the government proposed that the company should be nationalised. Northern and its BET parent company ran an aggressive campaign to remain private until the threat eventually receded. Ultimately however the company would be nationalised, but not for another twenty years.

Above: *Gateshead 75 - a Leyland Titan PO3-4, near Newcastle Civic Centre.*

In the meantime the company notched up anther first: the AEC Routemaster was being built for London Transport; Northern determined to have the best buses available bought 51 of them. One is still retained by the group today, a group which now also still runs many of London's remaining Routemasters.

Nationalisation in 1968 did not seem to have much impact at first. That changed through the 1970s: the subsidiaries disappeared from the road - though interestingly were not legally wound up. Many of Northern's vehicles were painted in National Bus Company red. Those that were not painted red were resprayed yellow because they now operated in the area of the Tyne and Wear Passenger Transport Executive.

In the late 1970s passenger numbers were falling, the private car was in the ascendancy and much of public transport was in the doldrums. Innovation locally centred on the north east's new Tyne and Wear metro.

Above: Optare Excel 8134 is one of the 43 purchased since 1997. *Right:* 449 is one of a batch of Optare Solo minibuses used to convert the Washington local services to easy access.
Below: DAF SB220GS/Plaxton 4862 seen prior to entering service in 1999.

Despite the general down turn as a business entity Northern however continued to be profitable and it soon had to face another revolution. In a reversal of the previous government's policy the National Bus Company under which Northern operated was now to be broken up and privatised. Northern's own management had great confidence that they could create an excellent business. On 7th May 1987 Northern re-entered the private sector, now owned by its own senior managers. The new company had already branded itself Go-Ahead Northern and that phrase became the company motto.

The travelling public soon noted that the previously dormant subsidiaries began to re-appear in various guises. Privatisation brought many new buses. At this time the Gateshead MetroCentre was built; Northern was invited to manage the new bus station there and a special bus service to Gateshead was inaugurated becoming famed as the 'X66 Supershuttle'.

It is, of course, the bus and its livery that the passenger sees, not the company that owns it. Buses have become increasingly comfortable in recent years. One of the latest trend in bus design is the low floor single-decker which offer much improved access to the disabled, elderly passengers or parents with young children. As it has been in its past the group has been quick with the new technology. London put the first of the new buses into service but in 1994 the north east's Go Coastline became the next company to do so and Go North East now runs one of the UK's largest fleets of low floor buses and was the winner of the Claudia Flanders Bus Industry award for accessibility.

The Supershuttle service earns its place in our tale, not just because the best buses were run on it, with the impressive DAF Optare Deltas appearing in 1988, but because its existence helped shape the most recent pages in the Northern story. The group was growing, looking outwards and expanding away from north east England. What had once been a single company within the BET and NBC groups was becoming a national group itself. As a result of expansion nationally the 'Northern' name was now restricted to a company based at the two original garages at Chester-le-Street and Stanley. Go-Ahead Northern was renamed the Go-Ahead Group for its stock market flotation in 1994.

In March 1995, adding another 225 vehicles to the company's fleet one of the north east's oldest, largest and most respected independents, OK Motors of Bishop Auckland with roots dating back to 1912, was purchased.

In a further development in 1997 the North East subsidiary addressed the issue of its image. The blue red and yellow colours of the highly successful MetroCentre Supershuttle were used as the basis of the new livery for the north eastern fleet. What 20 years ago was merely the Northern General member of the National Bus Company 20 years ago is now the powerful Go-Ahead Group, comprising, in the north east Go Northern, Go Gateshead, Go Wear Buses and Go Coastline these local operations all managed under the collective banner of Go North East.

This story began in the northern heartlands of Tynemouth and Gateshead. It ends however far from the north east. By 1999 of the company's ten key subsidiaries nine were in London and the south of England. The privatisation of London Transport Buses brought London Central and London General into the group. Three more southern bus companies are in the group: Brighton and Hove, the Oxford Bus Company and the Wycombe Bus Company. Each of those companies has a leading role in its own area and demonstrate the group's technical prowess. The Oxford Bus Company for example was the first in Britain to fit buses with catalytic converters and other equipment reducing emissions by up to 90 per cent.

The privatisation of the railways presented another opportunity for the group. In 1996/97 two franchises were gained covering Thameslink and Thames trains. Thames Trains works out of Paddington and covers the country as far out as Hereford and Stratford-upon-Avon. Thameslink runs between Bedford and Brighton and is strategically placed to benefit from the one Railtrack connection available across the centre of London and which is being developed as the 'Thameslink 2000' route.

Nor has development of the group stopped at British shores. Gatwick Handling is an aviation services company owned by the group which operates at four UK airports.

Things have certainly changed: today's youngsters can no longer leap off moving buses nor smoke their wild Woodbines, but at least kissing hasn't yet been banned on buses!

Above left: *178 low floor vehicles arrived in the late 1990s to bring easy access to everyone.*
Top: *3815 is one of 23 Volvo Olympians with Northern Counties bodies based on Tyneside from 1998.*

Steeling milk

Readers familiar with the West End of Newcastle of 10 years ago and before will recognise the name of White Bros Ltd.

For the best part of the 20th century the company operated first from Fife Street and then from Westgate Road and Corporation Street.

The firm of White Bros (Newcastle on Tyne) Ltd was established in 1884; its founders were not surprisingly, two brothers - George and Ernest White. A third brother, Alan, born in 1900 later joined the firm and continued to work in the business right up until his death in 1972.

The company was originally established to provide the farming community in Northumberland and Durham with dairy equipment, plumbing and electrical installations.

For 60 years the firm occupied 236 Westgate Road together with the stable block to the rear (in Corporation Street) from which the firm only moved in 1989.

There were five children in the White family the two girls Olive and Grace occupied the spare accommodation in the front terrace in Westgate Road until they passed away in the late 1960s.

For many years White Brothers produced a catalogue of their goods for distribution amongst the farming community; that document takes us back to the days before bulk milk tankers and industrial scale dairies. By the 1920s White Brothers were manufacturing their own products such as milk churns and separators whilst also making and selling such, now barely remembered items, such as hand bells for milkmen

Above left: *Tom Lowther who ran the company for 40 years.* ***Above:*** *Early White Bros products.*
Below: *Whites working on a farm on Kenton Lane in the mid 1950s. The backdrop is towards Newcastle Airport. The building to the left of the hayrick is still standing.*

...o ring in the street and their leather cash bags for them to keep their takings in.

Since the second world war two generations have grown up who have no recollection that doorstep deliveries of milk did not always comprise delivery in a milk bottle with a silver foil top. Fewer and fewer people now remember that once upon a time the milkman often came around wheeling a milk churn on a handcart. Back then the milkman, rather like today's rather noisier ice-cream vendor, rang a handbell to attract housewives who came out of their homes carrying a jug into which the milk would be poured. Given the many odd-sized pots and jugs which appeared, how did the housewife know she was getting a full pint for her money? The answer, as older readers will remember, is that the milkman had a variety of different sized ladles - a gill, half a pint, a pint and a quart - each bearing a government weights and measures stamp. The ladles could then be dipped into his churn to serve a standard, measured portion. Younger readers may recoil in horror at the thought of such apparently unhygienic practices - perhaps it was unhygienic but if so why did the milk back then taste like real milk not the weak, watery, chalky liquid we get today?

But hygiene aside, the milkman needed to buy his stamped imperial milk measures from somewhere and in this part of the world the supplier was White Brothers who could provide ladles of up to a gallon capacity and measuring pails of up to four gallons along with tripod and scales to measure and weigh milk in the dairy.

A copy of the company's 1923 catalogue lists many such hardware items for the dairy, it also however lists such items as pumps and hydraulic rams, portable farm engines and electric light installations, all of which act as pointers to a potentially more varied future.

In the 1950s the company moved into producing stainless steel equipment for the ice-cream industry, which was becoming very popular at that time.

Alan White in the latter part of his life moved the company more into the industrial side of the business believing, rightly as it turned out, that this was where the future of the company lay. It was however Thomas Lowther who had joined the company in 1936 at the age of 20 as a cost clerk who further developed the

Above: *The factory at 67 Corporation Street - now a car park. The front shop has now been now demolished and the terrace is now accommodation.*

company in the industrial sector eventually completing the move totally away from farming and into sheet metal. Thomas Lowther was destined to eventually become Managing Director and finally the owner of White Bros following Alan White's death.

Tom Lowther was still very active in the company until the age of 73. With the assistance of the firm's current Company Chairman and owner Peter Harding, Tom eventually moved the company to its present premises at Gosforth Industrial Estate. The old premises had been unsatisfactory from almost every conceivable point of view as they were very dilapidated and operations had to be carried out on different floors and levels as the site sloped steeply. What limited space existed was fragmented so that flowline production was impossible and the effective manufacturing space was totally inadequate to accommodate the growing and increasingly diversified workload. To add to the firm's problems access both to the site, and within it, was extremely difficult.

Peter Harding's plans at that time involved inward investment in modern machine and technology, investments, which have resulted in the successful

company we see today. White Bros have become the leading stainless steel sheet metal workers in the area.

The company now has state of the art computerised Radan CAD/CAM Amada CNC shear, pressbrakes, laser and punching machines. The company also takes pride in its ISO 9000 quality approval, Health & Safety and environmental policy. Recent improvements include a water treatment collection tank approved by the local water authority and used before waste chemicals are passed into the main drainage system.

The site was increased in size in 1994 and 1998 by the acquisition of adjacent premises to cope with the increasing demands of the business. A new polishing shop was created with dust extraction booths and a great deal of effort went into noise and vibration control. Investment continued more recently: a new polishing machine was introduced in 2000 which combines increased speed of production coupled with health and safely improvements for the firm's employees.

Other innovations continued throughout the 1990s. In 1995 White Bros introduced its first standard

product Liquisafe since the days of its catalogues for the farming community. Liquisafe, as its name implies, is a safe method of transferring chemicals between containers rather than the conventional dip tube method.

In 1997 White Bros acquired Stellex Ltd with a factory and offices based at Hadston in Morpeth, Northumberland. Stellex is a catering equipment manufacturer in stainless steel and other materials. The business was an ideal addition giving White Bros a major product line of its own which fitted well with its computer aided modern machinery.

The business now specialises in stainless steel, highly finished, quality sheet metal fabrications, mainly for the food and pharmaceutical industries. Customers are now to be found all over the UK rather than just the local area. In fact some products are now exported to Europe and America.

For many years thousands of Newcastle residents would unknowingly have had daily contact with White Brother's products as their wives and mothers collected milk poured into their jugs using the firm's

ladles. Today, equally unaware, thousands more will have regular contact with the firm, buying food which has been processed in plants furnished with the firm's equipment or eating in canteens and restaurants which have been outfitted using White Brothers' stainless steel fittings. Once again we can only pause for a moment to reflect that the story of a business, as much as that of individuals and families, is one with many twists and unexpected turns.

Below: *White Bros' premises today.*
Bottom: *Westgate Road in April 1989.*

The commercial estate that never just pottered

Wherever you went on Tyneside at one time it was not long before you came across one of the fleet of Hoult's furniture removal vans. Countless thousands of families had entrusted the safe transportation of family heirlooms from one home to another for over 65 years. No job was too small, no large contract so difficult that it could not be fulfilled. On that sort of reputation, a business empire was established. Branches were established up and down the country and abroad. There were offices in London and Germany. When there was a heavy army presence in the days of 'Two way family favourites' with Jean Metcalfe and Cliff Mitchelmore, there were three such offices to service the British Army on the Rhine (BAOR). Householders and businesses alike came to rely on Hoult's to send their goods speedily and safely on their way. There was even an instance of the firm having to move the whole contents of a castle across the Atlantic! Even to an accomplished and experienced firm, this was something of a logistical problem. However, with careful preparation and planning, the move was successfully executed. Other difficult moves were presented by offices

wishing to relocate. Every lost minute is lost business. Those companies were anxious to ensure that wasted moments were kept to a minimum. By strategic forethought and efficient delivery, Hoult's were always able to provide a more than satisfactory service. Working weekends and evenings made sure that the wheels of commerce or industry remained well oiled. If the customer wanted to move delicate or precious items, Hoult's provided specialist packing and handling services.

Right: Fred Webster and Geordie Tweddle with their new Leyland Tiger. *Below:* Hoult's maroon vans with the big white diamond were well known throughout the country.

So, if it was moving equipment of a multi-national, then the name of Hoult was the first one you reached for in the telephone directory.

Edward Hoult, however farsighted a man he might have been, would have found it difficult to picture the company today. In 1917 he opened for business in a little office on New Bridge Street. He had previously worked with Bainbridge's removal department. It was not the

easiest of times to set up a new business. War was raging. The last thing people thought of was moving house. They were staying put, waiting for loved ones to return from the front. However, Edward had timed it right, despite all the suggestions that the climate was wrong for such a venture. The armistice brought with it a sense of the pioneering spirit. Men who had not set foot beyond the edges of their home town before had been used to crossing continents during the Great War. Their wives had become familiar with the workplace as they kept body and soul together taking over jobs that had once been traditionally male. Families were soon on the move. During the next decade there would be a great population shift as work was chased up and down the land. The coming of the age of widespread motor travel, better roads and the increased efficiency and speed of the railway system all helped to widen horizons. What began as a small business with a horse drawn van, slowly moving around Newcastle, soon developed into a long distance removal business. Army surplus vans and wagons were made available to the general public. Many builders, funeral directors and haulage firms saw their opportunity and modernised their transport. In 1919, Edward Hoult bought his first motorised vehicle.

Early in the 1920s, large Leyland vans were whizzing along the A1. By then, Edward had recruited his three sons, Edward, James and Fred, into the business. Edward Jr was the admin buff, Jimmy looked after the maintenance of the vehicles and Fred handled the sales side of the firm. It was a true family enterprise. They did the lot. Many of their competitors still used the railways to transport people's possessions. But, the Hoult family soon established itself as the area's leading removal firm by their hard work and the commitment to the motor vehicle as the transport of the future. They were right. Before long, knowing that a speedy and efficient service was on offer, clients voted with their feet. They moved over to Hoult's.

Above: *The firemen's sense of humour!* ***Below:*** *Roll-on-roll-off ferries opened up the European market.*

By 1930 a garage had been opened on Northumberland Road, so large had the fleet of vehicles become. Always looking to the future, the Hoults formed an alliance with Union Transit Co of Glasgow. This helped open up the territory north of the border and forged a good working relationship between the two companies that continued for many years. Offices in Chelsea were opened and, in 1936, large warehousing facilities were opened in Southgate. This meant that there was now accommodation for the firm's vehicles in the south and a large amount of

storage space, that had been desperately needed, was made available. By now, household names like Harrods, Selfridges and Waring & Gillow were customers. This helped further the Hoult reputation even more. The head office moved to Newcastle city centre and the company continued to look to take over further premises to use for the growing storage market. More and more commercial removal business was taken on as the firm flourished. Edward Hoult senior died in 1941 and was succeeded by his three sons, Edward, Fred and James. In 1947 under the enthusiastic leadership of Fred, the firm took over the historic CT Maling Pottery on City Road. These extensive, but under used premises, were ideal for storage but Fred accepted the challenge of putting

the pottery back on the map. Maling Pottery had a long and illustrious history. The Maling family ran the North Hylton Pot Works near Sunderland in the 1760s. It was here that the art of transfer printing was established. Having exhausted the local clay deposits, the business moved to Tyneside and works at Ouseburn Bridge opened in 1817. The early introduction of mechanisation held the challenge of the Stoke potteries at bay. During the second half of the 19th century a new Ford pottery was producing jam and marmalade pots for Keiller's of Dundee and dishes for creams, ointments and potted meats. Another pottery was built and developed into the 20th century, keeping apace of fashion fads like art deco. Faced with challenges from glassware and plastics, with increased competition from overseas, especially Japan, Maling Pottery saw production drop away in the 1930s. During World War II government restrictions on all but utility pottery meant that the bad times became worse.

Top: *The 'Red Boy' by Reynolds moved for Lord Lambton, a regular customer.* ***Above:*** *Fred Hoult (left) with John Bennett (right) hold the tape for Vauxhall Managing Director to open the Cramlington garage.*

In 1961, Fred's son Fred, joined his uncle in the removal business and further expansion took place with branches opening in Glasgow, Nottingham and Germany to serve an increasing European market. In 1978, Fred bought out all the other share holders in an exciting management buy out.

But times change. The removal business was sold in 1983 to National Freight. The company, now Hoults Estates, concentrates its energies on being industrial property owners. Fred saw the need for secure storage and in particular, a thrust for self storage and set up Lock n' Store, a self storage company on the Maling site.

When Fred Hoult took up an interest, a remarkable recovery took place. He encouraged the designers to be bold and go for experimental designs. Production and exports rose. New equipment and increased optimism heralded a new dawn. Sadly, with Fred's death the revival faded. The company closed in 1963.

Three years after the purchase of the Maling Pottery site, the Hoult brothers were proud to buy the removal department of Bainbridges, the renowned departmental store where their father had worked, along with its modern warehouse in Higham Place. Sadly, Fred and James both died in the early 50s leaving Edward to run what was by then an extensive empire on his own.

It has been through listening to customer requirements and keeping an observant eye on modern business trends that the Hoult family has been able to develop its own business. This has seen it diversify from the original removal company into garage ownership, a brief spell into farming and back into consolidation of its commercial estate.

Further expansion and success for the firm looks set to continue with the completion of 30,000 square feet of factory units in the summer of 2000.

Top: *Two new BMC trucks outside the original Maling Pottery.* ***Above:*** *In 1970 shipping crates were unloaded on the quayside for shipment abroad.*

Putting the NEW (and the old) in Newcastle

If over a century in the building industry has taught Stephen Easten Ltd anything it is the inestimable value of a skilled and valued workforce. That concept has been the cornerstone of the company since its beginnings in the 19th century. Although today the term 'craftsmanship' has become somewhat debased, at Stephen Easten Ltd the word still retains its original meaning playing a key role within the permanent team of skilled staff.

Stephen Easten Limited was incorporated in 1906 although the firm's founder Sir Stephen Easten started his business some years earlier when at the age of 21 he left his home in Lowick a village south of Berwick upon Tweed and settled in Newcastle upon Tyne.

The future knight was born in 1867 and apprenticed to the building trade in Norham-on-Tweed. The young Stephen Easten went through some hard times before finding his feet in Newcastle as a builder. The new business began in 1888 and rapidly grew to important proportions. Stephen Easten was elected as a member of Newcastle City Council in 1906 and in 1917 was appointed Sheriff of the city. The pipe smoking bearded master builder was eventually to also serve twice as Newcastle's Lord Mayor.

Stephen Easten had made an excellent business decision in moving to Newcastle. In the following years the firm built many of Newcastle's most famous buildings and Stephen was eventually to be given an OBE and ultimately made a Knight of the Bath.

It was Sir Stephen's vision and enthusiasm which played a key role in the construction of both the original Newcastle Airport and the world famous Tyne Bridge - Sir Stephen was Chairman of the Joint Bridge Committee. It fell to Stephen Easten in his capacity of Lord Mayor to have the honour of welcoming King George and Queen Mary to Newcastle on 10 October 1928 to open the Tyne Bridge.

The company's project record is remarkable: in Newcastle's city centre there are many fine examples of the company's building expertise - Milburn House, Carliol House and the University Union Building, all constructed in the first half of the twentieth century, and all have stood the test of time.

The inter war years were some of the most important in the firm's history and that of Newcastle. At the time probably no other building in the North created more interest than the large building which was designed to accommodate the Newcastle upon Tyne Electricity Supply Company - Carliol House. The building with its 430 ft frontage to New Market Street was faced with Portland stone; the design of the facade with its domed corner and unbroken cornice was designed to be simple and dignified, relying on spacing and the proportion of the windows together with refinement of detail for its main architectural qualities. The walls of the main office were panelled in marble in which was set a bronze memorial in memory of the company's staff who died in the Great War.

Milburn House was erected on a triangular site with the apex of the triangle at its lowest point - the two sides being on two of the steepest inclines in Newcastle - Dean Street and The Side. On the site there still existed some of the oldest buildings in Newcastle in addition to many old walls and the original outside walls of the castle and the Black Gate.

Above: An early company letterhead.
Top left: Company founder, Sir Stephen Easten.

Enormous care needed to be taken in construction to prevent Newcastle Cathedral and the Black Gate from subsiding as the site was excavated. To cope, running sand excavations had to be dug down 40 feet, and 12 wide, to provide concrete foundations strong enough to bear the building's weight. The final building comprised five hundred rooms used as offices by over a hundred tenants. Modern construction techniques were used throughout: despite the red granite plinth and stone and brick facing the building was built around a steel-frame structure with all the walls being concrete although more traditional materials were used in the interior such as oak panelling and oak floorboards throughout the central halls whilst the staircase treads were of teak.

Similar care for detail was lavished on the College Union Building in Newcastle. The architects conceived it on the lines of one of the great houses built during the Elizabethan period and the style harmonised with other college buildings. A careful choice of materials was made to ensure the full qualities of the building would be realised in future years. The stone was Portland and that combined with soft-toned sand-faced bricks gave a mellowness and texture admired by all who appreciated a good building. The characteristic features of the period were found in the detailing inside the building.

Above: *Milburn House (Dean Street and Side) nearing completion.*

There is a vaulted corridor on the ground floor, an interesting oak-panelled room on the first floor and over the whole of the top floor clerestory lights which formed a pleasing finish.

Another significant work for Eastens in this period was the addition of two further storeys to the Tyne Commissioners' offices Newcastle upon Tyne. The harmonious addition of the two additional floors above the original main cornice was an early triumph of sympathetic building extension.

A similar early example of sympathetic change and restoration to an existing building was the Newcastle and Gateshead Gas Company's offices bounded by St John Street and Grainger Street. To carry out this very intricate and delicate operation all the internal brick walls were removed from the building and, pending the fixing of steelworks, the whole of the roof and towers were shored from the basement. Due to the difficult soft nature of the sub-soil special precautions had to be taken with the main foundations to the stanchions and it was decided to place these foundations on a reinforced concrete raft.

Eastens moved into the entertainment field during the 1950s carrying out major cinema conversion work for the Rank organisation throughout the United Kingdom.

The end of the 20th century saw the reconstruction of North Tyneside College including the addition of new lecture and engineering buildings.

Below: *Carliol House, Pilgrim Street.*

been involved in helping to restore Cross House to such a high standard.

The company has always believed that by retaining a nucleus of permanently employed craftsmen it can satisfy discerning clients and maintain the quality of service and finish which is synonymous with the Easten name. Today regular clients include banks, building societies, national retailers and numerous local authorities.

The firm currently employs over 100 people and continues to maintain the high standards set by its founder, recently scooping two out of six of the Lord Mayor's design awards given by Newcastle City Council and the Newcastle Initiative awarded biannually to firms which have designed and constructed buildings of outstanding excellence. Stephen Easten Ltd won the Special Conservation Award for the Alderman Fenwicks House project on Pilgrim Street.

David Sutherland the chairman of Stephen Easten finds it amazing that they should have received an award for the restoration of a house built three hundred years ago and hopes that in a hundred years' time their buildings will be lovingly restored by craftsmen.

Stephen Easten Ltd has developed a national reputation for refurbishing and restoring listed buildings in addition to

Also the construction of the award winning North Eastern Motors at Lemington incorporating the restored glassworks "cone", and the restoration and refurbishment of important buildings in Newcastle's Grainger Town.

One of Newcastle's most distinctive older office buildings, Cross House, emerged from a 1.2 million pound refurbishment with a new lease of life in an outstanding city location. The quality of the work on Cross House is a credit to the commitment of the owners, the architects and the contractors Stephen Easten Ltd. The task involved major structural work including replacing a huge concrete cross wall running to the full height of the building, with a steel frame to support the building's weight; in the process the Stephen Easten team found evidence of a disastrous fire that Cross House suffered in 1912. John Latimer, Stephen Easten's Contract director found it a fascinating project because the building is steeped in so much history, and he finds it a pleasure to see older buildings in the City being revived; the firm are particularly proud to have

Above: *Alderman Fenwick's House, Pilgrim Street.* **Right:** *Cross House, Westgate Road and Fenkle Street.*

undertaking more traditional building projects. The company is proud of its long history which is centred on the principles of skilled craftsmanship and quality workmanship.

That tradition of craftsmanship continues and, combined with modern construction materials and techniques enables Stephen Easten Ltd to provide a unique and responsive building service that is tailor-made to suit the needs of all its clients

Sir Stephen Easten's legacy of quality workmanship lives on helping to ensure that more than a century after its founding his building company continues to thrive.

Mounting the scaffold in safety

Scaffolding is an integral part of the building process, but when a building is completed and the scaffolding is dismantled it is only the professional scaffolder who can still see the telltale signs of the craftsmen who once erected that scaffold. The brickwork, joinery and tiling meanwhile remain for generations to see.

Scaffolding is an ancient skill handed down through the centuries. It is incumbent upon scaffolders today to uphold and maintain the skills and traditions of past masters. One firm dedicated to upholding that proud tradition is the Gateshead company Colmil Plant and Equipment. Comil provides an efficient and effective scaffolding service in a complex industry - one which imposes pressure on costs, where timeliness is critical to production and one in which safety is of paramount importance.

The commonest form of scaffolding in the Housing Market is the Putlog Scaffold. The name 'putlog' originated in Medieval times in the days when great castles and cathedrals were being built throughout Britain. In those long gone times timber scaffold poles were stood vertically and, at intervals, were roped together by a 'log' which was 'put' into a hole in the stonework. When the building was completed and the scaffold dismantled the 'log' which had been 'put' in the hole could not be easily removed and was sim-

ply sawn off flush with the wall. Over time the remaining wood rotted and a hole in the stonework appeared. 'Putlog' holes can still be seen today on many medieval castles and on other surviving buildings.

Today the Colmil Plant and Equipment Company based in Abbotsford Road, Felling, Gateshead is the name synonymous with scaffolding excellence in the North of England. Established over 40 years ago the company services the housing, construction and shipping industries throughout the North East, Yorkshire and the Midlands, offering a completely managed sub contract scaffolding service or individually-designed hire-only packages.

Colmil is dedicated to providing clients with a modern, efficient and effective scaffolding service utilising the skills of personnel trained by and registered with the Construction Industry Training Board. All Colmil scaffolders and managers are professionals directly employed by the company; they are proud of their ability to provide safe places of work.

The firm believes that statutory regulations regarding safety are wholly justified amidst the complexity of modern construction activity.

Above: One of the first orders placed by Colmil in November 1956 for the supply of scaffolding tube. **Right:** Scaffolding built by Colmil in the centre of Newcastle.

Above: *A scaffold contract carried out between December 1965 and March 1966 for the Kellogg International Corp. at ICI Wilton, Teesside.*
Top: *Scaffolding erected on Berwick Lifeboat Station. The scaffold was built off the concrete legs of the station due to the shifting estuary bed at the mouth of the Tweed. The work was completed on time despite high tides and rough seas.*

Colmil is committed to safety through training: their working foundation is British Standard 5973: 1993: Code of Practice. Safety is not open to compromises.

According to Managing Director Peter Hagen "...to produce a quality service for a client who places no limit on time and money is a relatively easy objective to achieve and is every supplier's dream....to do so in an industry which imposes pressures on costs, where timelines is critical to production and safety is of paramount importance is the reality Colmil has responded to, not by dreaming but by actively developing the reputation within a complex industry of being 'Simply the Best'."

The company was founded on 23 November 1956 and still retains its original logo of a scaffold-clad building. The business took its name from its two founders: Hughie Colquhoun and George Miles.

Hughie Colquhoun had previously been a scaffold manager whilst George Miles had been a promotions executive before they decided to start the new business venture together. From the beginning the new firm offered contracts for scaffolding and also hired and sold builders' plant and equipment.

The business was first based in a yard in Saville Place Newcastle - now part of Newcastle Civic Centre. The company remained there until 1968.

Hughie Colquhoun was the 'action man'. A well known personality in the construction world he was an exceptional controller of the work force. George Miles was the Sales Executive and administrator; equally respected for both his charm and professionalism.

In 1968 to accommodate an increasing workload and growing work force the company relocated to offices and a yard south of the Tyne at Abbotsford Road, Felling which had formerly been occupied by Structural Painters Ltd - later part of International Paints.

The scaffolding components used today have changed little in concept or design since the firm was founded in 1956; but quality standards and working practices have changed immensely in line with progressive and stringent safety regulations in the construction industry. Long gone are the days when the traditional breakfast for building site workers included refreshment in the form of a couple of bottles of brown ale!

One form of scaffolding though, now no longer seen in Britain, but which was being used by at least one of the North East's major house builders as late as 1973 was the traditional scaffolding poles lashed together with rope - a method of scaffolding going back over 2,000 years but today mainly seen only in such places as the Far East where bamboo poles are still a common scaffolding material.

Hughie Colquhoun and George Miles retired from the business in 1975 - Colin Herbert, who had joined the company in 1968, bought both their shares. George and Hughie have since sadly died. Colin Herbert retired in 1995 following a management buy out.

Between 1978 and 1996 the company expanded geographically into Yorkshire acquiring additional bases in Wakefield and the West Midlands at Brierley Hill near Wolverhampton.

The main challenge facing the company during the 1970s and 80s was to move away from dependence on industrial and heavy engineering related work and to establish its own niche market where the firm could gain a reputation for quality and service.

Although competition was there in abundance from smaller organisations - businesses which often had less concern for safety, training and direct employment of their workforce - the company began to concentrate its efforts in the rapidly growing housing market.

Top: Scaffolding supplied by Colmil for the application of a special maritime coating to the hull of the QEII in Southampton dry dock. *Above:* Colmil's offices on Abbotsford Road.

Some of the firm's competitors at the time were 'cash in hand' organisations and were just as problematic as the 'cowboy builders' who have received so much attention in more recent times.

Having researched the market however the company focused its resources on the house building market offering tailor made business packages to clients. Those packages included an all embracing concept of design, supply and control of scaffolding equipment which the client then rented on a hire basis and utilised his own scaffolders.

Colmil developed an in depth knowledge and understanding not only of scaffolding requirements in the house building industry but also of the construction techniques and working methods of all the individual trades involved in the production of a house.

Following the phenomenal growth of the housing market during the 1980s it collapsed 1989/90. Colmil however detected the early signs of a change in the building industry, particularly with regard to cost accountability and safety legislation. That foresight prompted Colmil to develop its sub contract scaffolding operations to the housing market taking total responsibility for the design, supply of materials and the provision of labour trained to recognised national standards of competence. Colmil succeeded in its aim whilst simultaneously retaining the firm's presence in the industrial market.

The number of people employed by Colmil has risen

from some 45 in 1990 to a current level of 125. The company firmly believes in, and is committed to, the

training of apprentice scaffolders. That training is provided in conjunction with the Construction Industry Training Board's apprenticeship scheme and in association with the National Access and Scaffolding Confederation. The company is currently training over 20 apprentices and anticipates this will increase year on year for some years to come. It takes two years to train a scaffolder to the current required levels of competence but according to Peter Hagen 'the best scaffolders of the future are those you are training today'.

Peter Hagen believes the company's future 'will now be one of controlled geographic expansion, concentrating our resources and skills in areas where we know we can be effective and having influence in matters concerning the safety of those individuals who rely on us to provide a safe working area to carry on their trade'.

Scaffolding has come along way since Medieval times. The modern 'putlog' is no longer a balk of wood but a short length of steel tube with one end flattened to enable it to be rested in the brickwork of a building as it is built.

In the North East however putlogs are often referred to locally by other names such as a 'spade end' or a 'fish tail' which are fair descriptions of their appearance.

Such names can however cause confusion. Peter Hagen recalls his days as an apprentice working his first week in the yard; he was about to go to the local shops at lunch time to get some 'bait' and asked the foreman whether he could get him something to eat as well. The foreman who was preparing a wagon load of scaffolding had not really been listening to the lad and told him he needed another fishtail. The young Peter Hagen disappeared to the shops without having given the foreman the putlog and returned ten minutes later with a 'tail end of fish and chips'. The foreman's response is not fit to print, but he ate the fish and chips!

One cannot help but wonder many master scaffolders working on our great castles and churches had similar experiences in their youths.

Left: Scaffolding around the former Princess Mary maternity hospital during its conversion into luxury apartments.
Above left: *Part of the Colmil transport fleet of 12 wagons and vans.*

Delivering the goods for over 80 years

The Newcastle based company, Simpson Brothers (Tyneside) Limited is today, one of the biggest names in the packaging transport business. However, this successful position was not perhaps inevitable from the start.

The company's founder, George Brumwell Simpson had always wanted to become a farmer. Despite his ambitions in this direction, George studied engineering and then worked as a farm manager. In 1919, in a tongue in cheek rebellion, he set up in business as a transport firm for farmers.

The new business was founded in Stocksfield and George bought two ex-army vehicles in order to carry out the work. In the early days this consisted of providing local transport for farm goods and building materials and delivering them from the local station to nearby houses and farms. George also carried out removals for 10 shillings a load and generally hauled anything and everything from furniture to hinds and shooting equipment!

The business soon took off and it was not long before George enlisted the help of his brother, Dick

Right: George Brumwell Simpson Junior.
Below: A very early line-up of the firm's fleet of lorries, pictured in 1920. George Brumwell Simpson is pictured left and Dick Simpson is on the right.

Simpson who he took into partnership thus establishing the company's name as, Simpson Brothers. The vehicles were then also used to collect coke from Stocksfield station in the Northumberland area and take it to the large country houses.

The Simpson Brothers' vehicles soon gathered a highly regarded reputation for their reasonable prices and for being the cleanest vehicles on the road. Indeed, this reputation is still upheld today even though the fleet has expanded somewhat!

In 1921 the fledgling firm was able to purchase a motor house which was erected by Ferrier Brothers Builders for £87. George's brother Dick left the firm after a few years. However, the business still remained within the Simpson family. After Dick's departure George was joined by his two sons, George and Ralph. Although grateful for their help, George continued to hold the reins of the business right up until his 87th year.

The decade of the 1930s got off to a promising start. In 1930 Simpson Brothers received its first major order. A contract was signed to haul milk from Stocksfield Creamery to Cumberland and Co-op shops throughout Northumberland and Durham. The 1930s continued as they had begun and in 1937, a garage site was purchased at Stockfield for £150. This was followed a year later, in 1938 when land was purchased from Lord Allendale at Stockfield for £146.6.6d.

The advent of the second world war brought with it upheaval for lots of businesses. Although George Brunwell served his country during the war, fortunately Simpson Brothers managed to carry on transporting farm goods as well as distributing milk from the local diary. At the cessation of hostilities the family firm resumed full operation once again.

Indeed, it was in the 1940s that the company's connection with the steel industry first began when work was undertaken for Steelworks in Jarrow. The number of vehicles was increased to four and the firm went on to gain work with the Blaydon based steel stockholder, Edward S Johnson and also with Kimberly Clark at Prudhoe.

The company's post war development was ever increasing but gradual. Throughout the decades of the 1950s and 1960s the firm continued to flourish, collecting more contracts and completing more and more work to the same standards of excellence instituted from the foundation.

By the 1970s the founder's sons Ralph and George were running the business and George was ably assisted by his wife, Joyce who looked after the administration side of the concern. It was during this decade in the year 1976, that George and Joyce experienced the proud occurrence of seeing their son, Peter Simpson becoming the third generation of Simpsons to join the family firm.

Above: *A milk lorry pictured in the 1930s.* ***Top:*** *From left to right are George Brumwell Simpson Jnr, driver Maurice Taylor and Ralph Simpson.*

93

Peter Simpson had started his working life as a fitter for another local company, Union Trucks. This time served him well and in 1976, with a total of five years experience under his belt, Peter joined the family business. At first, Peter worked as a driver and in the early days carried out a lot of work for BSC Jarrow. However, unlike his father before him, George gave Peter the scope to develop the business and allowed him to pursue his own ideas. In the event, this flexible approach paid off as it was mainly Peter's hard work and innovation that took the company forward at a rapid pace.

Peter progressed from being a driver to a manager and soon the firm became so busy that he was needed full-time in the office. Despite this, he still helps out from time to time with the driving and is not averse to cleaning the company vehicles in order to uphold the Simpson Brothers' excellent reputation. At the time Peter joined the business Simpsons had five vehicles and an annual turnover of £240,000. However, with his help this was to increase dramatically over the following years - the company was ripe for expansion.

During the decade of the 1980s this expansion came to fruition. Throughout these years a major invest-ment in terms of efficiency was implemented with the installation of the industry standard 'Road Runner' computer software. Once set up, the soft-ware made a considerable difference in the work of load and route planning. As well as this, efficiency and communication also improved when all the vehi-cles were fitted with in-cab telephones or band three radios. Another important development at this time was the transformation from flatbed trailers to cur-tain-siders with a capacity of more than 100cu.m. which are decked out in the firm's recognisable red and white livery.

Above: *A close coupled Volvo Drawbar, 1989.*
Top: *One of the early Volvo F86's pictured with George and Ralph Simpson in 1974.*

1985, Simpson Brothers was able to open a sec-
nd depot. Leeds was chosen as the location for the
ew depot as the company had already been carry-
ng out a lot of work there for steel distribution
ecialists ASD. Once settled in Leeds the firm won
usiness with plastic bottle manufacturer PetPlas
ackaging who produce drink containers for cus-
omers throughout the UK.

adly, in 1988, George Simpson died. However, the
eins of the family business were passed on to his
on, Peter's capable hands who carried the firm for-
ard with the assistance of his wife, Jean. Indeed,
he following year, 1989, was a landmark one in the
istory of the company. It was in this year that the
ompany celebrated its 70th anniversary.

owever, this was not the only event worth cele-
rating, Simpson Brothers also moved from its long
tanding premises in Stocksfield in this year to a
ew and larger base in Throckley, Newcastle. The
ew site was situated on the Westway Industrial
state and included the firm's own engineering and
aintenance facilities, 1,500 sq ft warehouse space
or storing dry goods and also had good access to
he North's major road systems. By this ground-
reaking year, Simpsons were operating the length

and breadth of the country with a turnover of £1.5
million, 24 lorries and 40 trailers.

At the end of the 1990s a recruitment company
called Simtemp was set up near Pontefract which
supplied the industry with skilled temporary drivers, forklift operators and warehouse workers.
Despite the popularity of the recruitment company,
Simpsons eventually closed the operation as people
were training with them and then leaving to work
for other companies.

Throughout the 1990s increased business from
PetPlas and Consett based Blowmocan allowed
Simpsons to forge ahead and increase vehicle num-
bers and turnover.

In 1999 the success continued when the firm won an
electrical based contract in Leicester worth half a million pounds. This was followed by more business in
the North East with Myson, a manufacturer of radia-
tors. By 1999 Simpson Brothers had 68 curtain sided
lorries, a turnover of £7.5 million and employed 80
drivers, and 20 office and workshop staff.

Today, the company continues to develop and is
now a member of the Transport Association, has a

260,00 sq ft warehouse space in
Pontefract split between four clients
and has staging posts in Leicester,
Milton Keynes and Leeds. The company specialises in high volume, low
weight products and logistic services
and also offers a quality distribution
service at a cost effective price.
Indeed, with the new generation of
Simpsons, the founder's great grand-
sons next in line to join the family
firm, Simpson Brothers is set to continue delivering the goods for many
more years to come.

Left: *Peter and Jean Simpson in 1996
with one of their Scania vehicles.*
Below: *One of the current fleet of lorries pictured in front of the Tyne Bridge.*

Flexibility is the watchword

In the 1960s the Animals used to sing a blues song 'I'm going to take you back to Walker'. Perhaps Eric Burdon and his chums were thinking of paying a visit to Walter Cox Ltd on Welbeck Road. Though basically a local business, it attracts customers from as far afield as Ashington, South Shields and Durham. This remarkable firm is known as a major electrical, furniture and carpet retailer. But that is not the whole story. It offers an amazing range of goods and services. There is a wide selection of leading brand names in the electrical world, various floor coverings that include carpeting, vinyl and laminates and a host of choices in the wood furniture department.

Added to these are the clothing section and the video library. But it does not stop there. In a veritable Aladdin's cave, customers can shop for prams and

pushchairs, Easter eggs and hampers with the occasional sunbed for good measure. Visitors are amazed by the variety and impressed by the speed of service. It comes as no surprise to learn that successive generations of shoppers continue to patronise the business.

Ever aware of client needs, Walter Cox Ltd has a cheque cashing facility, thanks to a good working relationship with Barclays Bank. As the number of High Street banks dwindles, this service is becoming more important. There is now a sister company, Walter Cox (Finance) Ltd that offers personal loans and gift vouchers for other major stores. The firm has continued to make sure that the smaller accounts are not forgotten.

*Above left: A page from a ledger dating from December 1940. **Below**: Walter and Ellen Cox at the wedding of Kathleen and David Cox on 6th October 1971.*

here is a home collection credit service. This can ad to some rib tickling moments. There has een more than one occasion when the agent has nocked on a door and been greeted by a little ne. When told that, 'Mam's ot in,' the collector always sks when she will return. Iaving said, 'I divvnt kna, ang on', the youngster gives ne game away by bellowing p the stairs, 'Mam, he wants) know when you'll be back'! Vhat mam does to her ffspring then is, fortunately, omething we had better not o into.

he firm has changed in style nd size since Walter Cox pened his first shop. He had een a watch and clock epairer before the 1914-18 var and was even involved in he manufacture of ships' chronometers. Walter ad been delayed in setting up his business by he outbreak of hostilities. Having served his ountry's army with distinction, he opened for usiness at 90 Church Street, Walker in 1918. Jsing the skills he had learned as an apprentice, Valter soon developed a fine reputation as a eliable horologist. The tools were basic. Cog vheels were cut by hand, a long and laborious rocess. The days of computer aided precision ool work were some way off. But craftsmanship as its rewards. In 1935 the company moved to 62 Welbeck Road and soon expanded further long the road, acquiring adjoining properties. Nowadays, there is also a warehouse that is used o carry large items of stock, such as suites, ables, wardrobes and other large pieces.

Valter Cox was a keen bowler and was often seen mparting thumb bias on his woods as they sped

across the greens at Walker Park and Millers Dene. His name lives on in the annual competition at Walker Park as the company sponsors this event. Links with those first days continue through the family involvement with Walter Cox Ltd. The founder's son, Douglas, who was born in 1919, followed in his father's footsteps. He served in the armed forces during the second world war and joined the firm on his demob. Douglas helped to expand the business by widening the range of the merchandise. When Walter retired he took over as managing director. He has now retired, in his turn. Walter's second wife, Ellen, bore him another son, David, in 1946. On leaving school, he joined the family concern and was a director at the tender age of 21. By 1984 he had taken over the reins of Walter Cox Ltd from Douglas and continued the company expansion. David's wife, Kathleen, and daughter, Samantha, are also heavily involved. Now linked to the internet, Walter Cox Ltd looks forward to taking care of its customers in both the traditional manner and via the new e-commerce.

> *In 1935 the company moved to 562 Welbeck Road and began a period of expansion*

bove: Cox's three shop fronts today.
Right: One of the displays from the carpet salesroom.

Leading the way with lead

A major European metals business which is still flourishing in Newcastle has its roots firmly based in the industrial history of the North East. That metal is lead.

Lead has been mined since antiquity and the extraction of Galena, the principal mineral in which both lead and silver are found, became a major industry in the North Pennines during the late 17th Century. The availability locally of this important metal was to give rise to many businesses in and around Newcastle.

In 1703 lsaac Cookson, son of a Penrith brazier, came to the city and set up ironworks, a colliery, salt pans and a glass works. His nephew, also named Isaac, moved to the area in 1720 and became one of Newcastle's most famous silversmiths. In 1742 he entered into partnership to mine lead ore in Teesdale.

Another partnership, that of Walker, Fishwick and Ward, leased two acres of land at Elswick in 1778 and was commissioned to de-silverise lead from the Cookson mines for use by Cookson's silversmiths. Walkers also started to manufacture sheet lead, white lead (for paint) and lead shot. The 192 foot shot tower completed in 1798 was to be a major Tyneside landmark for 170 years

refinery in 1851 and installing a new steam engine in 1855. Three more acres were added to the site in 1865.

By the middle of the Century the workforce had grown to 96 men, 45 women and three boys under 18 making it at that time one of the largest employers in the Newcastle area.

In 1884 the works had a 930 foot frontage on the Tyne and contained 33 white lead stacks, two sets of red lead furnaces, a "Rozan" steam de-silverising process, six hydraulic pipe presses and a 35 horse power beam engine.

The site also contained a number of workmen's cottages, a workers' dining room and bathrooms, and the Partners' house - a substantial building with gardens, stables, greenhouses and tennis courts well separated from the works.

Meanwhile the Cookson family, together with a partner William Cuthbert, had finally decided to become involved in lead manufacturing. In 1851 they set up lead and chemical manufacturing plants on land acquired at Hayhole and later Willington Quay. They also opened up a London office to improve marketing in the South of England.

The Company has remained active to this day and still manufactures sheet lead for the construction industry from its high technology operation based at its original Elswick location but now operating under the name of Calder Industrial Materials

During the 18th Century the Company prospered installing a new rolling mill in 1846, building four white lead stacks, slag hearths and a

Right: *Transportation at the end of the 19th century.* **Below:** *A panoramic view of the River Tyne with Calder's famous shot tower in the centre of the picture.*

which concentrated most of the Group's UK activities in Newcastle. However one example of a shot tower still exists at Calder's Chester factory, its future guaranteed as a listed monument.

The Elswick site still flourishes where it all began over 220 years ago. It is now the headquarters of the Calder Group, Europe's largest supplier of lead sheet and speciality fabricated lead products. A diverse range of markets are served including construction, automotive, chemical, medical, nuclear and steel industries. The Group operates from nine sites across five countries.

Sheet lead produced by the company has been used in prestigious buildings such as Royal Palaces, York Minster and closer to home most buildings in Grey Street as well as modern examples such as the Law Courts and Fenwicks.

The Cookson business proved to be immensely profitable providing in 1878 a return on capital of 25 per cent and furnishing Clive Cookson with an income of £42,000 in 1892. This compares with the average daily wage for women in the industry at the time of less than two shillings and five pence (12p) per day!

Despite this disparity both Cookson's and Walker's became noted for their conscientious and progressive attitude to workers' welfare introducing insurance schemes and medical facilities.

In 1949 the Walker and Cookson businesses together with eight other manufacturers joined forces under the name of Associated Lead Manufacturers. In recognition of the family's contribution to the business the Cookson name was adopted for the Group in 1984 with the Newcastle operations becoming known as Cookson Industrial Materials. Roland Cookson held an office at Elswick until his death in 1991 at the age of 82. Sadly there is no longer any member of the family associated with the company. A further ownership change in 1994 led to the current name of Calder Industrial Materials.

The shot tower was demolished in 1969 to make way for an extensive modernisation programme

Investment in the latest technology underpins Calder's position as leader in the lead industry. At Newcastle a state of the art rolling mill was installed in 1982. Further technological modifications were added in 1999 to increase production to 15 tons per hour of finished product, light years away from the early days of Isaac Cookson.

Above left: *The 192ft shot tower.* ***Top:*** *An aerial view of the works in the 1960s.* ***Below:*** *Modern technology at work - Elswick's computerised rolling mill.*

A smooth operation

From time to time most of us will use oil and grease. Perhaps we get out the oil can to fix a squeaking door hinge, grease the battery terminals under our car bonnet or give our garden tools a 'spring service'. One thing we probably do not do when we've finished the job and are wiping our hands on an old rag is think about where our oil might have come from, or indeed spare a thought for those who made that oil and the astonishing range of other lubricants such firms produce.

One company which could throw some light on our collective ignorance is the Newcastle firm of Revol Limited which has been manufacturing industrial lubricants for most of the 20th century. Revol lubricants are used throughout the world in many industries including; automotive, railways, shipping, oilfields, farming, defence, paper production, civil engineering, mining, steel production, power generation, textiles, engineering and even food production. Indeed it is difficult to find an industry which is not a user of Revol products!

Revol Limited is an independent manufacturer of speciality lubricants based in Newcastle Upon Tyne. The firm produces a wide range

Right: *William H Wilkes, one of Revol Limited's first sales representatives, pictured with his company car in the late 1930s.*
Below: *An exhibition stand at the British Industries Fair, Birmingham, 1937.*

of oils and greases, many containing solid additives such as Molybdenum Disulphide, Graphite, PTFE and soft non-ferrous metals that are used in a vast range of applications.

For the non-professional the world of lubricants can seem to be a complicated one. What for example is Molybdenum? A fair question and one to which Revol is happy to provide an answer: Molybdenum Disulphide (or Moly as it is known in the trade) is a naturally occurring mineral and is a compound of the elements Molybdenum and Sulphur with the chemical formula MoS_2.

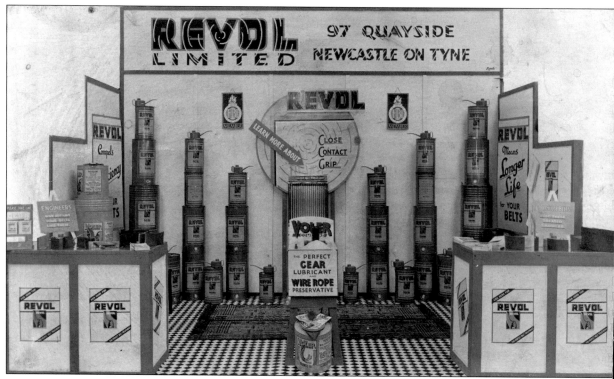

bearings and belts. Revol lubricants were marketed under the 'Voler' brand name which was chosen as an anagram of Revol.

In those early days the company had a select product range comprising predominately of Voler Compounds (open gear wire rope and chain lubricants) and Revol speciality products. By the 1960s James Arnott & Co had been acquired by the Burmah Castrol Group of companies and Revol Limited continued as a Specialities House within the group. Following a management buy-out in 1967, Revol became an independent company and moved into the purpose built factory at Killingworth, on the outskirts of Newcastle, where the business is based today.

The past thirty years have been a period of constant evolution for Revol Limited both in terms of the products manufactured and the diversity of markets now serviced as the company has

The lubricant grade of Moly is a powder which has a low co-efficient of friction - in other words it is a very slippery substance - the particles of which when introduced to a machine, become bonded to metal by a rubbing action and thus become deposited exactly where needed. By contrast PTFE is a man-made polymer (with the daunting name of PolyTetraFluoroEthylene) useful as a lubricant in high temperatures and ideal for 'clean' applications where other lubricants might be unsuitable.

"Perhaps we would be on safer ground simply asking what is grease?" But even that apparently simple question has a less than simple answer when asked of the experts. The vast majority of greases are based on two component parts: a base fluid and a thickener. To that base a third constituent of an additive package is often included, it is the selection and blending of these three components that keeps Revol in the vanguard of the lubricants industry.

Revol Limited was founded in 1926 as a specialities division of James Arnott & Co. Arnotts at that time was one of the oldest lubricant producers in the United Kingdom, having manufactured Arnoco Oils for over 100 years. The location of James Arnott's original oil blending works on the Newcastle Quayside is now the site of the Newcastle Law Courts. The Revol name was chosen as an abbreviation of 'Revolve' or 'Revolution' to emphasise the fact that the company's products were mainly to be applied on moving, revolving machine components such as gears,

reached out from its Newcastle base to be a global supplier of quality oils and greases. Today Revol is owned and managed by the Wilkes family, Ken and his sons Richard and David, their aim is to ensure that the firm's evolution guarantees the continuing smooth revolution of the world's industrial machinery.

Above right: *Picture taken circa 1950 from Newcastle Quayside. The lorry in the foreground belonged to James Arnott & Co and is liveried to advertise Arnoco Motor Oil.*
Above left: *'Big Geordie', the famous Dragline Excavator, which began work in Northumberland in 1969 and represents Revol's largest single lubrication project to date. 'Big Geordie' is now retired but several similar machines around the world still use Revol/Voler Lubricants.* ***Below:*** *The 21st century Newcastle Quayside. The building pictured houses the Newcastle Law Courts which are built on the site of James Arnott's original oilworks, from where Revol first traded.*

Driving north east business forward

Motoring has raced a long way since William Dalkin and Matt Turnbull joined forces to create The Wingrove Motor Company Ltd, back in June 1925. Those were the days of mudguards and running boards, semaphore indicators and real leather upholstery - and colour and style meant a choice of black or black!

With motor fuel in his blood (so to speak), William's son John Myers Dalkin - known to all as Jack - joined the business in 1927. Having been surrounded by cars from an early age, Jack developed a love for motor sports, joining both the Newcastle and District Motor Club and the Northumbria Motor Club. In 1954, during which year he also took on the role of managing director in the firm, he took part in the Monte Carlo Rally, repeating the experience again the following year.

Jack's own sons Brian and Peter, who as they grew up also become involved in the business, could scarcely avoid being infected with the same enthusiasm for speed and performance, and Peter became responsible for an offshoot of the Wingrove Motor Company, Perdal Developments. Making cars go faster was grist to Peter's personal mill, and he found himself receiving letters and requests from all over the world which ranged from two-shilling components to fully-tuned engines which sold for around £620. By the late 1960s Perdal's had an export turnover of £3,000 a month - and it was still growing.

Peter is now the managing director and he and his wife, Eunice, have three children, Lindsay, Elliott and Louise. Lindsay and Elliott are both involved with Wingrove Motor Company and Louise is married to Ian Parker who is employed by Lovekyns of Kingston, a large Citroen dealer in London. Ian and Louise have a son, Joshua.

Peter Dalkin has spent many years rallying and has competed in major European competitions as well as taking part in the Paris-Dakar Rally and the RAC Rally. He and Eunice have even completed the gruelling Route 66 across America.

Today the largest Citroen dealer in the UK, the Wingrove Motor Company are justifiably proud of the fact that their parts department stocks more parts than any other dealer in the United Kingdom. It carries over a quarter of a million pounds of stock at any one time, giving customers an excellent first pick from stock and guaranteeing they get a first class service. The company offers a comprehensive service, not only to Citroen owners but to drivers of any make of vehicle, with a 2.5 acre bodyshop and a 24 hour recovery service with staff who are trained to the highest standards. And with the Motorsport Department specialising in tuning and styling the Citroen Saxo, the company that has long been committed to pace and acceleration are still at the forefront and in the driving seat.

Right: *Peter Dalkin, MD.*
Below: *The premises in the late 1920s.*

Carrying coals from Newcastle

The firm of F Short & Sons stevedores, warehousemen and transport contractors long had its headquarters at Maritime Buildings in Newcastle's King Street.

Back in 1914 the firm's founder Frederick Short had worked for the Tyne Tees steamship company before deciding to branch out on his own as a master stevedore working in Newcastle quayside. In 1925 the business became a limited company.

Three generations of Shorts were to work for the company, one of whom, W Short found his own fame as a professional footballer for Leeds City shortly after the 1914-18 war.

During the firm's early years Frederick Short became the solely appointed Admiralty Stevedore, an association which was to continue for over 50 years.

The range of master stevedoring and master porterage offered eventually made the company one of the largest firms of contracting stevedores on the Tyne. The firm moved sulphate of ammonia, sisal, canned goods, fruit, machinery, newsprint and plywood at the Newcastle Quay and timber from the TIC Docks.

In 1956 the company introduced the first of its conveyor belt ship-loading equipment. By the end of 1963 the company had shipped over 750,000 tons of sulphate of ammonia from ICI and over 200,000 tons of other products.

The haulage side of the business was developed early and by 1929 the firm operated a nightly service between Newcastle and Hull which continued until 1949.

The years of the second world war were very active ones for the company. The haulage part of the business however was taken over by the government and not

denationalised until 1954 when the firm was able to reclaim its Hull depot.

Stevedoring was eventually terminated due to decasualisation of dock labour and the serious decline in general cargo at Newcastle Quay. Today the firm concentrates on road haulage, freight forwarding, and vehicle repairs services. The business relocated to Green Lane, Felling Industrial Estate, Gateshead in 1971.

F Short's strongest selling point is its ability to respond to customer requirements at a moment's notice. The company's business philosophy is to continue to be profitable, operate safely and grow - an aspiration which is likely to be achieved given its technical superiority and continual re-investment in the most up to date equipment.

Above: Delivering drums for shipment from No. 22 Wharf, Newcastle Quay. **Bottom left:** *The premises in 1973.* **Below:** *One of the company's articulated lorries en-route from the docks.*

A view of the quayside which was captured back in November 1975

Acknowledgments

Newsquest (N.E.) Limited, publishers of The Northern Echo,
and in particular Peter Chapman and Chris Dean-Watson

Other fine images have been reproduced courtesy of the Ward Philipson Collection

Bill Lancaster BA MA PhD FRHistS

Staff at the Local Studies Library, Newcastle

Thanks are also due to
Peggy Burns who penned the editorial text
and Steve Ainsworth for his copywriting skills